W9-DHN-054

Stitch by Stitch

Volume 8

TORSTAR BOOKS

NEW YORK · TORONTO

Stitch by Stitch

TORSTAR BOOKS INC.
300 E.42ND STREET
NEW YORK, NY 10017

Knitting and crochet abbreviations

approx = approximately
beg = begin(ning)
ch = chain(s)
cm = centimeter(s)
cont = continue(ing)
dc = double crochet
dec = decreas(e)(ing)
dtr = double triple
foll = follow(ing)
g = gram(s)
grp = group(s)
dc = half double
    crochet

in = inch(es)
inc = increas(e)(ing)
K = knit
oz = ounce(s)
P = purl
patt = pattern
psso = pass slipped
    stitch over
rem = remain(ing)
rep = repeat
RS = right side
sc = single crochet
sl = slip

sl st = slip stitch
sp = space(s)
st(s) = stitch(es)
tbl = through back of
    loop(s)
tog = together
tr = triple crochet
WS = wrong side
wyib = with yarn in
    back
wyif = with yarn in front
yd = yard(s)
yo = yarn over

A guide to the pattern sizes

		10	12	14	16	18	20
Bust	in	32½	34	36	38	40	42
	cm	83	87	92	97	102	107
Waist	in	25	26½	28	30	32	34
	cm	64	67	71	76	81	87
Hips	in	34½	36	38	40	42	44
	cm	88	92	97	102	107	112

Torstar Books also offers a range of acrylic book stands, designed to keep instructional books such as *Stitch by Stitch* open, flat and upright while leaving the hands free for practical work.

For information write to Torstar Books Inc., 300 E.42nd Street, New York, NY 10017.

Library of Congress Cataloging in Publication Data
Main entry under title:

Stitch by stitch.

Includes index.
1. Needlework. I. Torstar Books (Firm)
TT705.S74 1984   746.4   84-111
ISBN 0-920269-00-1 (set)

98765432

© Marshall Cavendish Limited 1984

Printed in Belgium

All rights reserved. No part of this publication may be reproduced, stored in any retrieval system, or transmitted in any form or by any means, electronic, mechanical photocopying, recording or otherwise, without the prior permission in writing of the Publishers.

ISBN 0-920269-08-7   (Volume 8)

Step-by-Step Crochet Course

Step-by-Step Knitting Course

Contents

Crochet / COURSE 34

*More filet crochet
 techniques
*Shaping a garment
*Pointed filet lace
*Pattern for a filet dress

More filet crochet techniques

In this course we show you how to increase and decrease the blocks and spaces used to make a filet crochet fabric. You can use this method of shaping to create a zig-zag edge, which is very attractive worked along the bottom of a filet garment or as a separate filet edging. Borders and edgings worked this way make ideal trimmings for many household items, including sheets and pillowcases, where the border can be sewn on the material after it has been completed. Why not try your hand at this technique? You could work an edging for a lace bedspread to give a really luxurious finish, or perhaps make a deep lace border for a summer dress or petticoat in fine crochet cotton.

Shaping a garment

Although this method can be used to shape a garment where the fabric is worked entirely in filet crochet, the steps created by decreasing or increasing a complete block or space on each side of the fabric would be too steep when used in conjunction with a thick cotton yarn or knitting yarn.
It is better to confine this kind of shaping to a garment where the fabric is worked in a fine crochet cotton with a small mesh pattern. For example, where the basic filet mesh has only one chain worked between the doubles to form the spaces, as shown here.
The patterns can be shown in the form of a chart (see Crochet course 33, Volume 7, page 22). Once you have mastered the very simple method of increasing and decreasing the blocks and spaces, you will be able to combine all you have learned so far to create your own borders, edgings and filet patterns for summer tops, dresses and many other garments and household items.

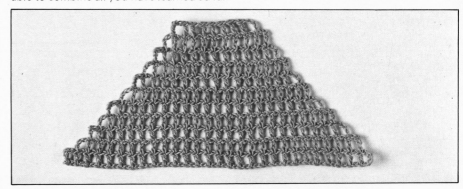

Increasing a space at each end of a row

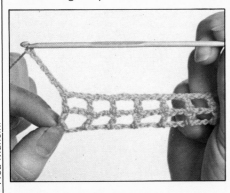 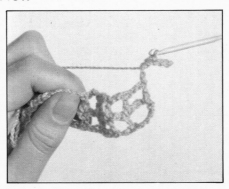 

1 Before you can work the increase row, you will have to work additional chains at the beginning of the previous row for the space to be increased at the end of the next row. Work 7 chains before you start to work the row preceding the increase row. For a smaller mesh, where 1 chain is worked between the doubles, make 6 chains; for a larger mesh where 3 chains are worked between the doubles, make 8 chains.

2 Now turn. Skip the chain nearest to the hook and work a slip stitch into each of the next 3 chains. These 3 slip stitches will form the basis for the additional space worked at the end of the next row. The last 3 chains count as the first double of the row.

3 Now make 2 chains. Work the next double into the next double of the previous row to make the first space. Continue to work in the correct pattern until you reach the end of the row, working the last double into the 3rd of the 5 turning chains in the normal way. Now make 7 chains. These chains will count as the first double (3 chains), 2 chains at the base of the row and 2 chains for the first space.

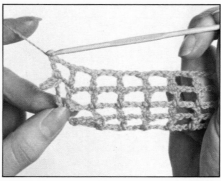

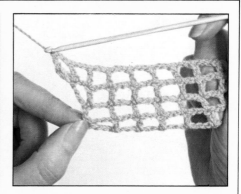

4 Turn and work 1 double into the first stitch of previous row, thus increasing one space at the beginning of the row. This space is now part of the pattern and should be worked as such on subsequent rows.

5 Continue to work in pattern until you reach the end of the row, working the last double into the turning chain as before.

6 Now work 2 chains. Skip first 2 slip stitches worked at the beginning of the previous row and work 1 double into the last slip stitch, thus making an extra space at the end of the row.

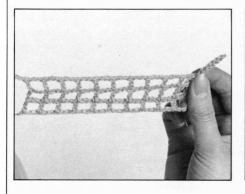

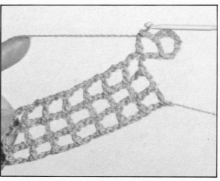

7 To increase 2 spaces at each end of the row you should work an additional 3 chains at each end for the 2nd space so that you work 10 chains in all, instead of 7 with a slip stitch worked into the 2nd to 6th chain for the spaces to be added at the end of the row.

8 Now turn and work the first double into the 8th chain from the hook so that the first 7 chains count as the first double and 2-chain space as before. Now work 2 chains and work a double into the top of the first (edge) stitch at the beginning of the next row for the 2nd space.

9 To work 2 spaces at the end of the row, work a double into the turning chain as before. Now make 2 chains, skip the next 2 slip stitches and work a double into the next stitch to make the first space. Work a further 2 chains and work another double into the *last* slip stitch for the 2nd space.

Increasing a block at each end of a row

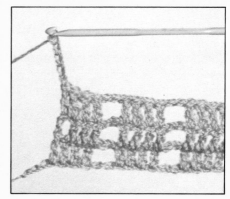

1 You need to work additional chains at the beginning of the row preceding the increase row for the block to be increased at the *end* of the row, by making 7 chains. When you are working a mesh with only 3 doubles in each group, make 6 chains, and for a block with 5 doubles work 8 chains.

2 Now turn and slip stitch across the 2nd, 3rd and 4th of these 7 chains, leaving the last 3 chains to count as the first double of the next row as before.

3 Continue in pattern to the end of the row, working the last double into the turning chain in the normal way. Now make 5 extra chains. Make 1 less chain for a 3-double block and 1 more chain for a 5-double block.

continued

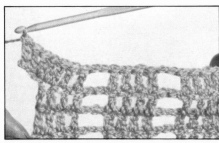

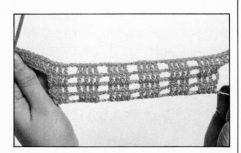

4 Now turn and work a double into the 4th chain from the hook so that the first 3 chains count as the first double. Now work a double into the next chain and first double (edge stitch) to complete the first block of 4 stitches.

5 Work in pattern to end of row. Now work 1 double into each of the 3 additional slip stitches to complete the last block. The double worked at the edge of the row counts as the first double of the block.

6 To increase 2 blocks at each end of the row, work 3 additional chains at each end for the 2nd block, working a slip stitch into the 2nd to 6th of the 10 chains when making provision for the block to be worked at the *end* of the row. On the next row work the first block as before then 1 double into each chain and first double of the row to make 2 blocks (7 doubles). At the end of the row work into the turning chain as before and then work a double into each slip stitch to make the 2 blocks.

Decreasing a space at each end of a row

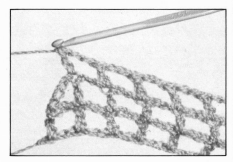

1 Work 1 chain at the beginning of the row where space is to be decreased. Now skip first double and work a slip stitch into each of the next 2 chains, followed by a slip stitch into the next double, so that you have worked over the top of the first space.

2 Work 5 chains to count as first double and 2-chain space. (Work 3 chains if a block is to be worked next.) The last double of the next row will be worked into the 3rd of these 5 chains in the normal way.

3 Continue across the row in pattern until 1 space remains unworked. Now turn and leave the remaining space unworked. The last double worked now counts as the first double of the next row. To decrease 2 spaces work in exactly the same way, leaving 2 spaces unworked instead of 1.

Decreasing a block at each end of a row

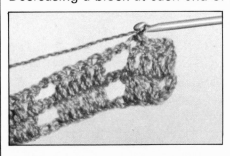

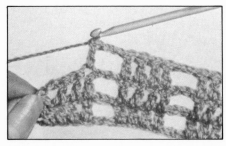

1 Make 1 chain instead of 3 at the beginning of the shaping row. Now skip the first double and work a slip stitch into each of the next 3 doubles so that you have worked across the top of the first block. Decrease 2 blocks by working in same way across 2 blocks instead of one.

2 Work in pattern until 4 doubles remain unworked at the end of the row. Now work a double into the next double.

3 Turn and leave the remaining 3 doubles unworked, so that you have decreased a block. The last double worked now counts as the first double of the row. To decrease 2 blocks leave 6 doubles unworked at the end of the row.

Fred Mancini

Pointed filet lace

Here we show you how to work a simple filet pattern from a chart, where 2 blocks are increased each time on one side of the fabric and then decreased in the same place on the other side of the work to form the point. By making a series of points in this way you can create a pretty lace edging. Try working two samples: the first using a thick cotton yarn or knitting yarn (knitting worsted would be suitable), so that you can become familiar with the working method, and then make the second sample in a fine crochet cotton so that you can see how effective filet crochet is when worked in this way.

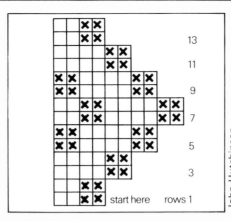

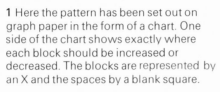

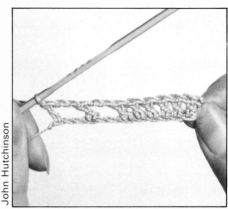

1 Here the pattern has been set out on graph paper in the form of a chart. One side of the chart shows exactly where each block should be increased or decreased. The blocks are represented by an X and the spaces by a blank square.

2 Each block in this sample consists of 4 doubles, so that you will need to work 7 doubles in all when working 2 blocks consecutively. Similarly each space consists of 2 chains with a double worked at each side. Begin by making 15 chains. Work the first row of the chart reading from right to left.

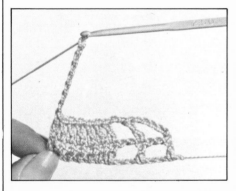

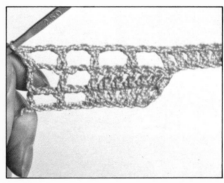

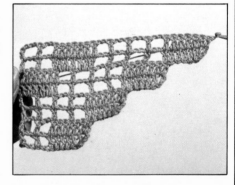

3 Now turn and work the 2nd row of the chart from left to right so that in this case you will work 2 spaces followed by 2 blocks as in the first row. Now work 8 chains in preparation for the 2 extra blocks to be increased at the beginning of the next row.

4 Turn and work a double into the 4th chain from the hook followed by 1 double into each of the next 5 chains. Work the last double into the top of the first double in the next row to complete the 2 blocks.

5 Continue to work in pattern from the chart, reading each right side row (uneven numbers) from right to left and each WS row (even numbers) from left to right, increasing 2 blocks where indicated until the 8th row has been completed.

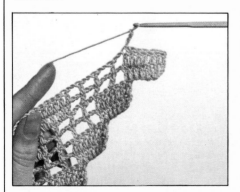

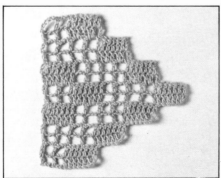

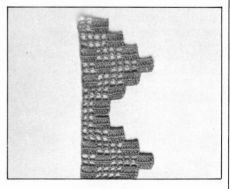

6 Now turn and decrease the first 2 blocks of the next row by working in slip stitch across the first 2 blocks, as shown in the previous step-by-step directions.

7 Continue in pattern reading each row in the same way as before until the last row of the chart has been completed.

8 Here we show you the same pattern worked in a very fine crochet cotton. Two points have been worked by repeating all the rows of the chart twice. You could, of course, repeat the pattern as many times as you like.

7

Party special

This girl's party dress has delicate filet crochet on bodice and hem. The hemline band is shaped to give a scalloped effect.

Sizes
To fit 24[26:28]in (61[66:71]cm) chest. Length, 23½[27:31]in (59.5[68.5: 78.5]cm).
Sleeve seam, 3½[4:4½]in (9[10:11]cm).
Note Directions for larger sizes are in brackets []; if there is only one set of figures it applies to all sizes.

Materials
9[10:11]oz (240[280:300]g) of a sport yarn
Sizes B, C and E (2.50, 3.00 and 3.50mm) hooks for 1st and 2nd sizes
Sizes C and E (3.00 and 3.50mm) hooks for 3rd size

Gauge
10dc to 2¼in (6cm) on size E (3.50mm) hook.

Back
Using size B[B:C] (2.50[2.50:3.00]mm) hook make 66[74:74] ch for lower edge of bodice.
Base row 1dc into 6th ch from hook, *1ch, skip next ch, 1dc into next ch, rep from * to end. Turn. 31[35:35] sp.
1st row 3ch to count as first dc, *1dc into next sp, 1dc into next dc, rep from * to last sp, 1dc into last sp, 1dc into next ch. Turn.
2nd row 4ch, skip first 2dc, 1dc into next dc—sp formed at beg of row, 1dc into each of next 2dc—block (blk) formed, work *3sp, 1blk, rep from * to within last 2dc, 1ch, skip next dc, 1dc into top of 3ch. Turn. Beg row 3 of chart, cont shaping neck as indicated. Fasten off. Using size C (3.00mm) hook make 3ch, with RS facing, work 60[60:62] sc along ch edge of bodice, make 5ch, turn.
Next row 1dc into 4th ch from hook, 1dc into next ch, then work 1dc into each sc across bodice, 1dc into each of the 3ch. Turn. 66[66:68] dc. Change to size E (3.50mm) hook.
Patt row 3ch to count as first dc, 1dc between 1st and 2nd dc, *1dc into next sp between dc, rep from * to end, working last dc into sp between last dc and 3ch. Turn.
This row forms patt. Patt 1 more row.
Shape skirt
Inc row 3ch, 1dc into next sp between first and 2nd dc, (1dc into next sp between dc) 15 times, 2dc into next sp—1dc increased—patt to within last 18dc, 2dc

into next sp—1dc increased—patt to end. Patt 3 rows.
Rep last 4 rows 8[10:11] times more. 84[88:92]dc. Cont straight until skirt measures 11½[15:18½]in (29[38:47]cm).
Shape lower edge
Next row Patt 37[39:41] dc, turn and cont on these 37[39:41] dc only.
Next row Sl st over first 8dc, patt to end. Turn.
Next row Patt until 8dc rem unworked, turn. Rep last 2 rows once more. 7[9:11] dc rem. Fasten off.
Skip center 11dc, rejoin yarn into next sp, 3ch, patt to end. Turn. 37[39:41] dc.
Next row Patt until 8dc rem. Turn.
Next row Sl st over first 8dc, patt to end. Turn. Rep last 2 rows once more. 7[9:11] dc rem. Fasten off.

Front
Work as for back, but follow chart for front bodice.

Sleeves
Using size E (3.50mm) hook make 16ch for top edge.
Base row 1dc into 4th ch from hook, 1dc into each ch to end. Turn.
Next row 3ch, 1dc into first dc, 1dc into sp between first and 2nd dc, *1dc into next sp between 2dc, rep from * to end, working 2dc into last sp. Turn. (2dc increased). Rep last row 8[9:10] times more, making 5ch at end of last row. Turn. Place a marker at top of last row.
Next row 1dc into 4th ch from hook, 1dc into next ch, 1dc into next dc, *1dc into next sp between dc, rep from * to end, working last dc into sp between last dc and 3ch, now using a separate ball of yarn sl st into top of 3ch at end of row and make 3ch, then fasten off. Return to end of row just worked and work 1dc into each of the 3ch. Turn. 38[40:42]dc. Patt 2 rows.
Next row 3ch, 1dc into first dc, 1dc into sp between first and 2nd dc, *1dc into next sp between dc, rep from * to end working 2dc into last sp. Turn. (2 dc increased). Rep last 3 rows 2[2:3] times more. 44[46:50]dc. Cont straight until sleeve measures 3½[4:4½]in (9[10:11]cm) from marker.
Next row 3ch, 1sc between 2nd and 3rd dc, *3ch, skip next 2dc, 1sc into next sp, rep from * to end, working last sc into top of 3ch. Turn.
Next row Work 4sc into each ch loop. Fasten off.

Filet hem (make 2)
1st size only
Using size C (3.00mm) hook make 31ch.
Base row 1dc into 5th ch from hook, 1ch, skip next ch, 1dc into next ch, 1ch, skip next ch, 1dc into each of next 3ch, *(1ch, skip next ch, 1dc into next ch) twice, 1ch, skip next ch, 1dc into each of next 3ch, rep from * once more, (1ch, skip next ch,

1dc into next ch) twice. Turn.

2nd size only
Using size C (3.00mm) hook make 34ch.
Base row 1dc into 6th ch from hook, 1ch, skip next ch, 1dc into each of next 11ch, (1ch, skip next ch, 1dc into next ch) twice, 1ch, skip next ch, 1dc into each of next 11ch.
Next row 1sp, 3blk, 5sp, 3blk, 1sp, 1ch, now dec 1sp by leaving last loop of each on hook and working 1dc into last dc and 1dc into 3rd of 4ch, yo and draw through all 3 loops on hook. Turn.
Next row 3ch, skip first dc and sp, 1dc into next dc, 2 sp, 1blk, (3sp, 1blk) twice, 2sp. Turn.

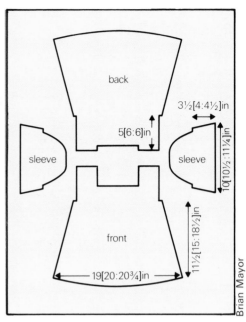

Brian Mayor

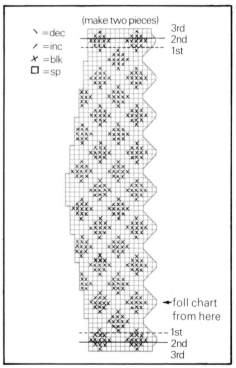

(make two pieces)

\ =dec
/ =inc
x =blk
□ =sp

3rd
2nd
1st

←foll chart from here

1st
2nd
3rd

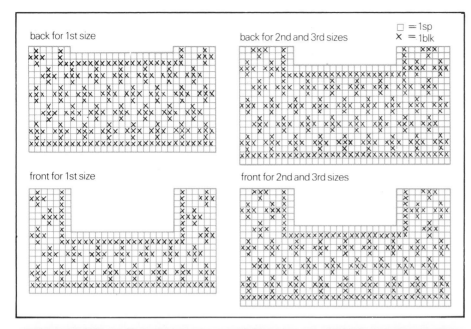

back for 1st size

back for 2nd and 3rd sizes

☐ = 1sp
✕ = 1blk

front for 1st size

front for 2nd and 3rd sizes

3rd size only

Using size E (3.50mm) hook make 32ch.

Base row 1dc into 6th ch from hook, 1ch, skip next ch, 1dc into next ch, 1ch, skip next ch, 1dc into each of next 3ch, (1ch, skip next ch, 1dc into next ch) 7 times, 1dc into each of next 2ch, (1ch, skip next ch, 1dc into next ch) twice. Turn.

Next row 1sp, 3blk, 5sp, 3blk, 2sp, now inc 1sp at end of row by working 1ch and 1dc into top of 3ch. Turn.

Next row 2sp, 5blk, 3sp, 5blk. Turn.

Next row 1sp, 3blk, 5sp, 3blk, 1sp, 1ch, now dec 1sp by leaving last loop of each on hook and working 1dc into last dc and 1dc into 3rd of 4ch, yo and draw through all 3 loops on hook. Turn.

Next row 3ch, skip first dc and sp, 1dc into next dc, 2sp, 1blk, (3sp, 1blk) twice. 2sp. Turn.

All sizes

Next row 5sp, 3blk, 3sp, 1ch, dec 1sp by leaving last loop of each on hook and working 1dc into each of next 2dc, yo and draw through all 3 loops on hook. Turn.

Next row 3sp, 5blk, 4sp. Turn.

Next row 5ch, turn, then work 1dc into first dc—1sp increased at beg of row—5sp, 3blk, 4sp, inc 1sp at end of row. Turn.

Next row Inc 1sp at beg of row, 2sp, (1blk, 3sp) 3 times. Turn.

Next row 2sp, 3blk, 5sp, 3blk, 1sp, inc 1sp at end of row. Turn.

Beg foll chart, from row marked. After center section has been worked dec 1sp at left side edge by skipping last sp of row as shown on chart. Fasten off.

To finish

Press lightly. Join shoulder seams.

Neck edging

With RS facing join yarn to corner dc at right-hand side of back bodice and using size C (3.00mm) hook work *3ch, skip next sp, 1dc into next sp, rep from * around neck, end with 1sc into sl st.

Next round Work 4sc into each loop. Fasten off.

Armhole edgings (alike)

With RS facing join yarn to beg of armhole and using size C (3.00mm) hook work *3ch, skip next row end, 1sc into side of dc of next row end, rep from * around armhole. Fasten off.

Next row Rejoin yarn to first st of last row and work 5sc into each loop. Fasten off. Set in sleeves, leaving armhole edging free. Join short ends of hem, then sew hem to lower edge of skirt. Join side and sleeve seams.

Lower edging

With RS of work facing join yarn to side of dc on first row of hem and using size C (3.00mm) hook work *3ch, 1sc into side of dc of next row, rep from * around lower edge, sl st into same place as join.

Next round Work 3sc into each loop. Fasten off. Press seams and edgings lightly.

Gary Warren

Crochet / COURSE 35

Weaving on crochet fabrics

In this course we show you how to weave yarn through a basic crochet net to make a warm textured fabric, which can be striped, checked or plain. It is ideal for rugs, afghans and many outdoor garments. You can either work the background in a striped pattern, then use one or more of the colors to work the weaving, or make the background in one color and use contrast colors for the weaving.

In general, yarns as thick as or thicker than knitting worsted give more satisfactory results than finer yarns.

The weaving is worked with either a large-eyed needle or safety pin. If the yarn is too thick to be threaded onto a needle, use a crochet hook.

Background fabric

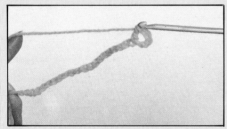

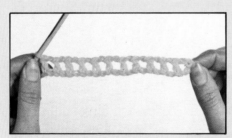

1 Begin by making an even number of chains. For our sample we have made 26 chains, using a knitting worsted and size G (4.50mm) hook. It is important to make sure that the fabric is worked evenly. If you find that the spaces are being worked too loosely to make a firm fabric, change to a smaller hook. Work 1 double into the 6th chain from the hook.

2 Now make 1 chain, skip the next chain and work a double into the next chain to make the 2nd space. Continue to work doubles and 1-chain spaces in this way all across the row, working the last double into the last chain. The 5 chains worked at the beginning of the row should be counted as the first double (3 chains), 1 chain at the base and the first 1-chain space.

3 On subsequent rows work a double into each double of the previous row, with 1 chain worked between each double for spaces. Begin each row with 4 chains, which should be counted as the first double and 1-chain space, and work into the 2nd double of the previous row. End each row by working the last double into the 3rd of these 4 chains so that the 4th chain counts as the last 1-chain space.

Weaving the yarn through the basic net

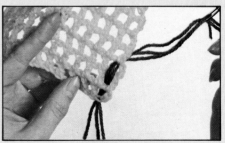

Fred Mancini

1 Cut three strands of yarn in a contrasting color so that they are approximately 4in (10cm) longer than the base fabric. The strands should overlap each end by 2in (5cm). The number of strands will depend on the type of yarn being used—with a bulky yarn you may only need to use 2 strands.

2 Trim the ends of yarn so that all 3 strands are the same length to facilitate the weaving. Thread all 3 strands onto a large-eyed needle or safety pin. Pass the needle and yarn through the middle of the base chain of the first space at the bottom right-hand corner of your work, so that the strands are held securely.

3 Now begin to weave the yarn, working in and out of the 1-chain spaces vertically up the length of your fabric. Take the yarn under the first horizontal chain bar. Now take the yarn over the next chain bar and under the following one, so that you are weaving the yarn over and under these bars each time.

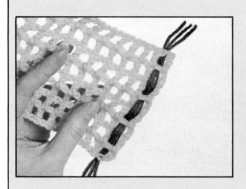 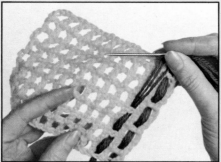 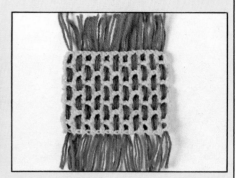

4 Continue to weave in this way, until you reach the top edge of the fabric. Now take the yarn through the middle of the top chain to hold the yarn securely at this side of the work. The loose ends can also be trimmed and left to form a fringe if you are making a rug or afghan.

5 Begin the next row of weaving at the base of the fabric, securing the yarn to the foundation chain of the 2nd space in the first row of the net fabric. Now take the yarn *over* the next horizontal bar and under the following chain bar so that you are weaving in the opposite direction to the first weaving row.

6 Continue to work up the 2nd row until it has been completed and the yarn secured at the top as before. Now repeat these 2 weaving rows until all the spaces have been filled and the last row worked. Make sure that you do not pull the yarn too tightly when working the weaving so that the fabric does not become distorted.

Weaving with a crochet hook

To make a sample like the one shown here use a bulky knitting yarn. Make the background in a striped pattern, working 2 rows in each color, then use the same 2 colors on every other row for the weaving to make this attractive pattern.

1 Cut and trim 3 strands of yarn in the same way as for needle weaving. Lay the yarn over the top of the fabric with the short ends extending over the edge of the fabric at the base. Now insert the hook from the back to the front through the middle of the base chain of the first space, at the bottom right-hand corner.

2 Wind the yarn tightly over the hook and draw it through the middle of the chain, to secure the yarn at the base of the fabric in the same way as when weaving with a needle. Make sure that the 3 strands are lying flat at this stage and have not become twisted while being drawn through the chain.

  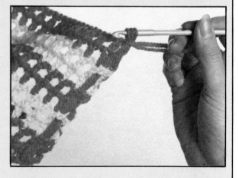

3 Keeping the yarn on top of the work, insert the hook from back to front through the first space and hook it over the three strands of yarn.

4 Draw yarn through to the back. Hold the yarn against the back of the fabric. Insert the hook through the next space from front to back and draw the yarn through to the front, holding the strands woven through the previous space with the left hand to maintain tension.

5 Continue to weave in and out in this way until the top of the row has been reached. Now insert the hook through the middle of the last chain bar and draw the yarn through to secure it firmly at the top edge of the fabric.

continued

11

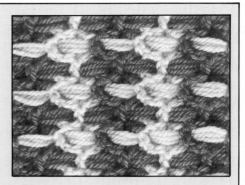

6 On the next row work in exactly the same way, using the 2nd color and reversing the position of the weaving. Begin the row by taking the yarn over the base chain bar and under the following bar.

7 Continue to work up the 2nd row alternating the position of the weaving each time, so that you are working in the opposite direction to the first row. Secure the yarn at the top of the fabric in the same way as before.

8 Continue to repeat the first and 2nd weaving rows alternately, changing the colors on every row until all the rows have been worked to complete the fabric. Using the same two colors for both the background and weaving is what creates this unusual texture.

Horizontal and vertical weaving

Here we show you how to work the weaving both vertically and horizontally onto the basic net to create the zig-zag effect. We have used one color in a knitting worsted for the background and two contrasting colors in a bulky knitting yarn for the weaving, but you could, of course, use knitting worsted for the weaving too if preferred.

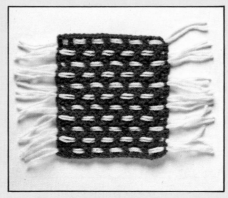

1 Make the basic net as given in the step-by-step instructions, page 10. Using 2 strands of bulky yarn in the first contrast color, weave the strands horizontally across the fabric, working in exactly the same way as when weaving vertical stripes, but working from side edge to side edge instead of from bottom to top.

2 Now begin to work the vertical lines, using the 2nd contrast color in bulky yarn. Secure the yarn to the base of the first space at the bottom right-hand corner of the fabric on the WS.

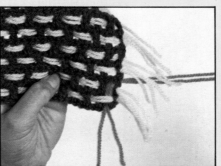

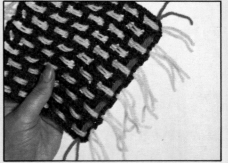

3 Now take the yarn under the first vertical woven stripe and bring it to the front again between this stripe and the next horizontal chain bar.

4 Now take the yarn over the next chain bar and woven stripe, and to the back again between this stripe and the next chain bar.

5 Continue to weave in this way, under and over the horizontal chain bar and woven bar together, all the way up the fabric, securing the yarn at the top as before.

Fred Mancini

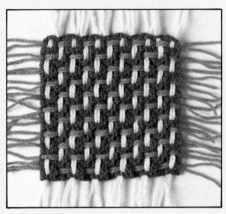

6 Now work the 2nd row of vertical weaving. Secure the yarn to the 2nd space at the bottom of the fabric and begin the row by taking the yarn over the first horizontal woven stripe and under the next chain bar and woven stripe, bringing the yarn to the front again between this stripe and the next chain bar.

7 Complete this row, working the weaving and securing in the sequence as now set, so that the yarn is taken over and under the chain bars and horizontal stripes in the opposite direction to the first row.

8 Now continue to repeat the first and 2nd weaving rows, using the same color for each row, taking care to weave the yarn over and under both a chain bar and woven stripe each time until all the rows have been completed to achieve the zig-zag effect.

Fred Mancini

Woven for warmth

Choose soft colors for the woven poncho overleaf, or vivid colors for a much brighter look. Wear it as an extra layer on chilly days.

Sizes
Width, 37¾in (94cm).
Length, 36½in (92.5cm).

Materials
25oz (700g) of a knitting worsted in main color (A)
3oz (75g) in 1st contrasting color (B)
2oz (50g) in 2nd contrasting color (C)
Size G (4.50mm) crochet hook
One button

Gauge
19sts to 4in (10cm) in patt on size G (4.50mm) hook.

Back
Using size G (4.50mm) hook and A, make 154ch.
Base row 1dc into 6th ch from hook, *1ch, skip next ch, 1dc into next ch, rep from * to end. Turn.
Patt row 4ch, skip first dc and work *1dc into next dc, 1ch, rep from * to end, finishing with 1dc into top of ch. Turn. This row forms the patt. Cont in patt until work measures 15¾in (40cm) from beg.
Shape lower edge
Next row Sl st to 2nd dc, 3ch, *1dc into next dc, 1ch, rep from * to within turning ch, turn. Patt 1 row.
Rep these 2 rows 13 times more, then work the first of these 2 rows 14 times. Fasten off.

Front
Using size G (4.50mm) hook and A, make 58ch. Work base row as for back, then patt 3 rows. Make 16ch at end of 1st row, cont.
Next row 4ch, 1dc into first dc, 1ch, cont in patt to end.
Next row Patt to end.
Rep last 2 rows twice.
Next row 15ch, work across ch as for base row, then patt across last row. Cont without shaping in patt until work measures 9in (23cm) from beg; end at armhole edge. Fasten off and leave aside. Make another piece in same way, but do not fasten off. Turn.
Next row Work to end, make 9ch at neck edge, then patt across first piece.
Next row Patt to end of first piece, (1ch skip next ch, 1dc into next ch) 4 times, 1ch, patt to end of second piece. Turn. Complete to match back.

Lower borders (alike)
Join A to shaped edge of poncho and using size G (4.50mm) hook work a row of sc evenly along shaped edge. Work in hdc for 2in (5cm). Fasten off.

continued

Brian Mayor

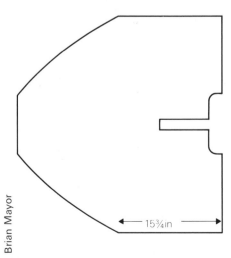

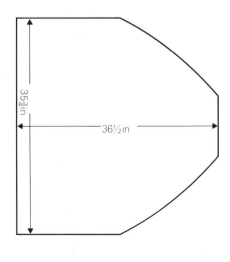

35¾in

36½in

15¾in

Marcus Wilson-Smith

13

Neck borders

Join A to left side of front opening and using size G (4.50mm) hook work a row of sc evenly along this edge. Work in hdc for 2in (5cm). Fasten off. Join A to right side of front opening and using size G (4.50mm) hook work a row of sc evenly along this edge. Work in hdc for 1in (2.5cm); end at top edge.
Buttonhole row 2ch, 1hdc into next hdc, 2ch, skip next 2hdc, 1hdc into each hdc to end. Turn.
Cont in hdc until band measures 2in (5cm) from beg. Fasten off. Join shoulder seams. Sew down front borders, lapping right over left. Work 3 rows of sc evenly around neck.

Armhole borders (alike)

Join A to outer edge of lower border and using size G (4.50mm) hook work a row of sc evenly along edge of border, straight edge of poncho and edge of other border. Sl st into first sc to join the pieces. Cont in rounds, working in hdc until border measures 3in (7.5cm). Fasten off. Sew on button to top of left front border.

Weaving

Using 2 strands of yarn weave vertical stripes in a sequence of 3 rows B, 2 rows C and 1 row A across both back and front. Darn in ends neatly. Press lightly.

Stitch Wise

Alternate mesh fabric with weaving

This pattern combines blocks of 3 doubles linked by a single double worked between each block. By changing the position of the blocks and single doubles on each row you create an open fabric as shown here. The pattern is worked over a multiple of 6 plus 5 chains. We have made 29 chains for our sample, using a knitting worsted yarn and size G (4.50mm) hook.
1st row 1dc into 4th ch from hook, 1dc into next ch, *1ch, skip 1ch, 1dc into next ch, 1ch, skip 1ch, 1dc into each of next 3ch, rep from * to end of row. Turn.
2nd row 3ch to count as first dc, skip first dc, 1dc into next dc, *1ch, skip next dc, 1dc into next 1-ch sp, 1dc into next dc, 1dc into next 1-ch sp, 1ch, skip 1dc, 1dc into next dc, rep from * to end, 1dc into top of turning chain. Turn.

3rd row 3ch to count as first dc, skip first dc, 1dc into next dc, *1dc into next ch sp, 1ch, skip next dc, 1dc into next dc, 1ch, skip next dc, 1dc into next 1ch sp, 1dc into next dc, rep from * to end, 1dc into top of turning chain. Turn.
The 2nd and 3rd rows form the pattern and are repeated throughout, noting that a half block and 1 space are worked at each end of the 2nd row every time to keep the pattern correct.

Either you can use the pattern above by itself, or you can weave three strands of knitting worsted horizontally in and out of the fabric to achieve the brick effect shown above.
Alternate the position of the weaving on every other row, so that you begin the first row at the right-hand edge of the

fabric, taking the yarn under the first three double block and then over the first single double, bringing the yarn to the front through the first chain space; then continue to weave across the row in the sequence as now set. On the 2nd row start from the right-hand edge again and bring the yarn to the front between the first and 2nd doubles, over the 2nd double and behind the first block, taking the yarn to the back through the first chain space. Then continue to weave across the row in the same sequence. By repeating these 2 rows each time you create the brick effect.

Here we show you the reverse side of the pattern, which gives an equally attractive woven effect.

Fred Mancini

Crochet/COURSE 36

*Open-lace patterns
*Solomon's knot
*Working Solomon's knot
 on a foundation chain
*Chain mesh
*Picot mesh
*Pattern for an evening
 shawl and bag
*Pattern for three bags

Open-lace patterns

There are many open-lace stitches which can be worked in crochet, combining stitches and large spaces to produce a really light, airy fabric which is both easy to work and quick to make. The patterns are ideal for making beautiful lace shawls and can be worked in a variety of yarns including any fine knitting yarns, mohair or any of the metallic yarns available today. For delicate garments, you will obtain the best results if you work with a fairly light yarn, rather than a yarn with a firm texture. Try working the patterns in something sturdier like a thick cotton yarn or string to make a really practical shopping bag.

In this course we show you how to work two of the most traditional of these stitches. The first one, Solomon's knot, employs quite a different method of working which, once mastered, is rather intriguing; the second is a basic chain mesh with a picot variation which would make a simple lace fabric for a summer top or shawl. As always with crochet you should try working the stitches in a variety of yarns—any odds and ends you have will do when experimenting—to see the different effects which can be achieved with these simple stitches.

Solomon's knot

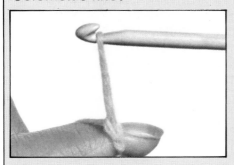

1 To create a really lacy fabric, this stitch can be worked without a foundation chain so that the edges remain soft and light. Begin by making a slip knot on the hook in the usual way and then a single chain. Now extend this chain, drawing it out so that it is about ½in (1.2cm) in length to make a neat, even fabric. If you draw the loop out farther you may find the resulting fabric too loose and uneven.

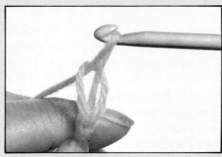

2 Now wind the yarn over the hook and draw it through the top of this loop, extending the yarn to the same height as the first chain. You will find it easier to draw the yarn through if you hold the first chain with the left hand.

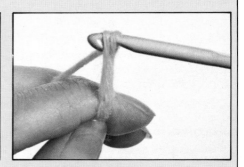

3 Hold the base of the loop just made with the left hand and insert the hook under the vertical loop from right to left so that both the original chain and this loop are now on the hook.

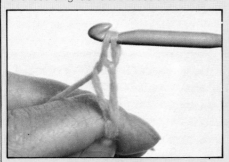

4 Now wind the yarn over the hook and draw it through the loop so that there are 2 loops on the hook and all the extended strands of yarn are held together at the top.

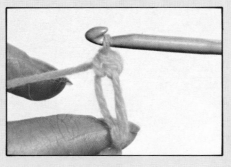

5 Now wind the yarn over the hook and draw it through these 2 loops to complete the first Solomon's knot or stitch. Thus each stitch consists of 3 loops with a single crochet forming the knot at the top to hold the loops together.

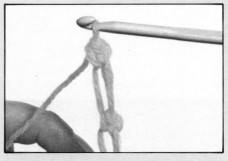

6 To make a 2nd Solomon's knot or stitch, extend the loop now on the hook to the same height as before and complete the knot in exactly the same way, repeating steps 2–5.

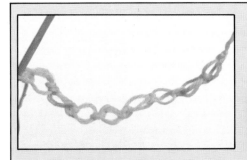

7 Continue to make as many knots as you need for the width of fabric you are making. We have made 8 knots so that, including the slip knot and chain made at the beginning of the row, we have made 9 knots in all.

8 To work another row, begin working from right to left in the normal way. Skip the knot nearest to the hook and the next *three* knots, and work a single crochet into the center of the next knot. It is important to make sure that your hook passes through the center of the knot and not just under 1 loop of yarn to ensure that the knots are joined firmly.

9 Now extend the loop on the hook and work 2 more knots in the same way as before. Skip the next knot in the previous row and work another single crochet through the center of the next knot. In this way you begin to build up the pattern.

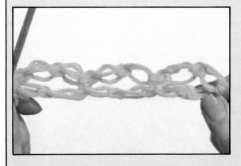

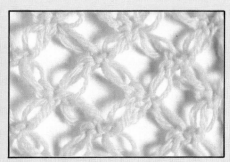

10 To continue working across the row, repeat step 9 each time and finish the row by working the last single crochet into the single chain made at the beginning of the first row.

11 To continue the pattern, work in the same way on every row, beginning each row by making three knots and working the first single crochet into the first *unjoined* knot in the previous row and then continuing to make 2 knots and work a single crochet into each unjoined knot across the row.

12 To complete each row work the last single crochet into the unjoined knot after the last *joined* knot worked in the previous row. Here we show you the completed sample, showing the characteristic 4-petal daisy effect created by working in this way.

Working Solomon's knots on a foundation chain

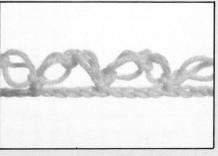

1 To make a firmer edge to your fabric, work Solomon's knot on a foundation chain, with a turning chain worked at the beginning of each row. First make a number of chains divisible by 5 (our sample uses 25). Then draw the loop on the hook out and work 1 Solomon's knot as before to start the row, followed by a slip stitch into the 10th chain of the foundation chain.

2 Now make 1 chain and work 2 more Solomon's knots before working a slip stitch into the 5th chain from the last slip stitch worked, thus skipping 4 chains between the slip stitches.

3 Continue to work 2 knots and a slip stitch into every following 5th chain across the row, working the last slip stitch into the last chain. This forms the base row of the pattern.

continued

Fred Mancini

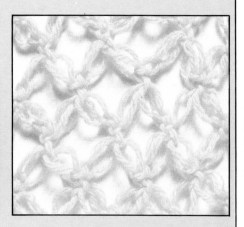

4 To continue working in rows, turn the work in the usual way and make 6 chains (for the turning chain at the edge of the fabric), and then make 1 knot to start the row.

5 Now work a single crochet into the first unjoined knot worked in the previous row. Continue working across the row, making 2 knots and working into unjoined knot of previous row. Work last single crochet into final turning chain worked before first knot in previous row.

6 To work the completed sample as shown here, repeat steps 4 and 5 several times, starting with 6 chains on every row to form the firm edge of the fabric and working the last single crochet into the 6th of these chains each time.

The photographs above, showing samples in sport yarn, mohair and string, illustrate the versatility of this stitch.

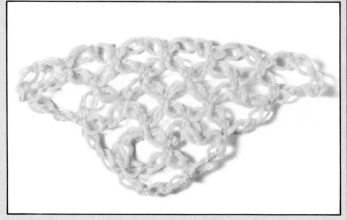

Because of the way a Solomon's knot pattern is constructed the shaping must remain fairly simple. However, you can decrease quite easily by skipping a knot at the beginning of every row. To decrease more gradually skip a knot at the beginning of every other row or even every 3rd or 4th row, depending on the shape you wish to achieve.

Similarly, when increasing it is simply a question of working an extra knot at the beginning of either every row, or every 2nd or even 3rd row, depending on whether you wish your fabric to increase sharply or gradually.

Chain mesh

This is one of the simplest lace stitches which can be worked in crochet, since the pattern is made by working lengths of chain, joined by a single crochet, to form the diamond-shaped mesh. The pattern can be worked in any kind of yarn, from a fingering yarn for a very fine light and lacy fabric to a thick cotton yarn or string for a shopping bag or beach bag. You can also alter the size of the mesh by working either more or fewer chains each time. If you are making something like a shopping bag, bear in mind that the mesh will stretch when the bag is in use, so the mesh should not be too widely spaced.

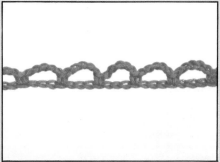

1 The pattern is worked over a number of chains divisible by 4 plus 1. For our sample we have made 33 chains but you can work as many chains as required for the width of fabric. Work a single crochet into the 9th chain from the hook.

2 Now make 5 chains, then skip next 3 chains in the foundation chain and work a single crochet into the next chain to make the 2nd loop. The first 9 chains will count as the first loop. Continue to work 5-chain loops with a single crochet worked into every 4th chain. Work the last single crochet into last chain.

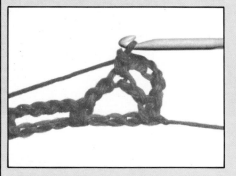

3 To work the next row, make 5 chains to start the row and then work a single crochet into the first 5-chain loop, working into the 3rd of these chains.

4 Now continue working a 5-chain loop and a single crochet into each 5-chain loop in the previous row, working the last single crochet into the center of the last 5-chain loop.

5 Each row is worked in exactly the same way as the last to complete the pattern as shown here.

Picot mesh

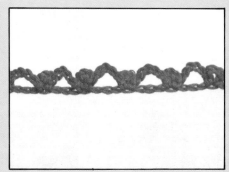

1 To work a simple variation on chain mesh, work a picot in the center of the chain loop. Begin the pattern in exactly the same way as when working the chain mesh and then make a picot in the 9th chain from the hook by working a single crochet, 3 chains and a single crochet all into this chain.

2 Now continue to work 5 chains and a picot into every following 4th chain across the row, working one single crochet into the last of the foundation chains, omitting the picot at the edge of the fabric.

3 Now turn and work 5 chains followed by a picot into the center of the first and every 5-chain loop made in the previous row, but working a single crochet into the center of the 3rd chain in the last loop. Each row is worked in the same way, omitting the picot at the end of every row to keep edges of fabric straight.

Fred Mancini

Midas touch

Accessories worth their weight in gold—this glamorous shawl and bag will give you a look of luxury.

Sizes
Shawl, length at center when hanging 37½in (95cm).

Materials
6oz (170g) of a thin gold metallic yarn
No. 0 (2.00mm) steel crochet hook

Shawl

Using No. 0 (2.00mm) hook make 6ch.
Base row Work 1 Solomon st (see page 16), sl st into last ch. Turn.
Next row 1ch, work 2 Solomon sts, sl st into last st. Turn.
Next row 10ch, work 1 Solomon st, sl st into center st between next 2 Solomon sts, 1ch, work 2 Solomon sts, sl st into last st, 1ch, work 2 Solomon sts, sl st into same st (increase made). Turn. Cont to increase in this way, working 10ch at beg of rows and (2 Solomon sts) twice at end of rows until 109 Solomon sts have been worked in a row.
Next row 10ch, sl st into center st between first 2 Solomon sts, *6ch, sl st into center st between next 2 Solomon sts, rep from * to end, sl st into top of turning ch. Fasten off.

Fringe
Using four 9in (23cm) lengths of yarn tog knot fringe along two side edges.

Bag
Using No. 0 (2.00mm) hook make 80ch. Work in Solomon's knot patt (see page 16) for 9in (23cm).
Next row Sl st into center st of each Solomon st. Cut off yarn, leaving a long end, thread end through all sts in last row, gather tightly and secure, then join seam. Do not block.

Cords (make 2)
Using No. 0 (2.00mm) hook make a ch 17½in (44cm) long, sl st into 2nd ch from hook, sl st into each ch to end. Fasten off. Thread cords in and out of spaces formed by patt, 2in (5cm) from top edge. Tie cords tog at each end to form handles.

Gary Warren

Bags of fun

Brighten up your day with these colorful and versatile bags made in wrapping twine.

Pink bag
Sizes
Width, 23½in (60cm). Length, 14in (36cm).

Materials
4 x 100yd (90m) of a lightweight unpolished wrapping twine
Size F (4.00mm) crochet hook

Using size F (4.00mm) hook make 110ch. Cont in Solomon's knot patt (see page 16) for 31½in (80cm).
**Next row 10ch, sl st into first Solomon st, *5ch, sl st into next Solomon st, rep from * to end, finishing sl st into top of turning ch. Turn.
Next row Work 1sc into each Solomon st, work 5sc into last st. Turn.
Next row 1sc into each of next 4sc, *2ch, skip next 2sc, 1sc into each of next 3sc, rep from * to end, finishing 1sc into last sc. Turn.
Next row 1sc into each of next 4sc, *2sc into next sp, 1sc into each of next 3sc, rep from * to end, finishing 1sc into last sc. Fasten off.**
Join yarn to foundation ch and work from ** to **. Fold in half lengthwise; join sides.

Strap
Using size F (4.00mm) hook make 200ch (or number of ch for length of strap required).
Base row 1sc into 3rd ch from hook, 1sc into each ch to end. Turn.
Next row 2ch, 1sc into each sc to end. Turn.
Rep last row once more. Fasten off.
Sew each end of strap to side seams of bag. Do not block.

Cord
Make a ch approx. 70in (176cm) long, sl st into 3rd ch from hook, sl st into each ch to end. Fasten off. Thread cord through holes at top of bag. Tie a knot in each end.

Green bag
Sizes
Width, 11in (28cm). Length, 19in (48cm).

Materials
2 x 100yd (90m) of a lightweight unpolished wrapping twine
Size E (3.50mm) crochet hook
One pair of bamboo handles, diameter 6¼in (16cm)

To make
Using Size E (3.50mm) hook make 45ch. Cont in Solomon's knot patt (see page 16) for 43in (110cm).
Next row 10ch, sl st into first Solomon st, *5ch, sl st into next Solomon st, rep from * to end, sl st into top of turning ch. Fasten off. Fold bag in half lengthwise and join side seams, leaving 7in (18cm) open at top. Do not block. Overcast top of bag to handles.

Yellow bag
Sizes
Width, 12½in (32cm).
Length, 10in (25cm), excluding handles.

Materials
2 x 100yd (90m) of a lightweight unpolished wrapping twine
Size E (3.50mm) crochet hook
One pair of wooden bag handles with 11in (28cm) slot

To make
Using size E (3.50mm) hook make 70ch. Cont in Solomon's knot patt (see page 16) for 21in (54cm).
Next row 10ch, sl st into first Solomon st, *5ch, sl st into next Solomon st, rep from * to end, sl st into top of turning ch. Fasten off. Fold bag in half lengthwise and join side seams, leaving 2½in (6cm) open at top. Overcast top of bag to handles.

Flower-rings

Make something pretty for your table with ribbons and flowers. These napkin rings are perfect for a tea table.

Finished size
2½in (6cm) in diameter.

Materials for each ring
2½in (6cm)-diameter child-size plastic bracelet
Small bunch of fabric flowers and two leaves
⅝yd (.5m) of narrow satin ribbon
Matching sewing thread

1 Wind the ribbon around the bracelet. Where the ends meet, leave about 4in (10cm) loose and sew together.
2 Arrange the flowers and leaves in a small bouquet. Wind thread tightly around the stalks, and tie to secure.
3 Tie the excess ribbon around the stalks and tie into a bow.
4 Snip the ends of the ribbon into V shapes to neaten and prevent fraying.
5 Repeat steps 1 to 4 to make other napkin rings.

Crochet / COURSE 37

*Fine crochet edgings
*Yarns and hooks
*Washing and blocking
*Sewing the edges onto your fabric
*Lace-shell edging
*Stitch Wise: more lace edgings
*Pattern for lace edging for sheet and pillowcase

Fine crochet edgings

Many people are reluctant to even try to work fine crochet. They believe that these patterns are far more complicated than anything they have tried before, simply because they are worked with a fine hook and fine crochet cotton to create the delicate lace effect. Of course the stitches you make will be much smaller than when working with a

knitting worsted and size G (4.50mm) hook, for example, so that you will need to work carefully and patiently. The actual stitches used, however, are exactly the same whether you are working a lace pattern in knitting worsted or fine crochet cotton, so provided that you read and follow the directions carefully you will be able to work fine lace edgings in a variety

of pretty patterns without difficulty.
The edgings can be used to trim all kinds of household items, including sheets, pillowcases and tablecloths as well as many garments, and you will have the satisfaction of knowing not only that you have created a beautiful lace fabric but also that it will have been made at a fraction of the cost of purchased edging.

Yarns and hooks

Traditionally these fine edgings were worked in pure white cotton thread and used to trim white table and bed linen. Today, however, colored sheets, pillowcases and tablecloths are popular, and the color range of crochet cottons has been extended enormously so that you should be able to match almost any colored fabric with a suitable cotton thread.
Here we show you the range of hooks used for fine crochet, together with the crochet cotton which is suitable for use with each hook. The thread ranges in size from a very fine No. 60, used in conjunction with a No. 14 (0.60mm) steel hook, to a medium thread, No.3, used in conjunction with a No. 0 (2.00mm) steel hook.

Hook	Crochet cotton
No. 14 (0.60mm)	60
No. 12 (0.75mm)	50
No. 10 (1.00mm)	40
No. 8 (1.25mm)	30
No. 7 (1.50mm)	20
No. 4 (1.75mm)	10
No. 0 (2.00mm)	3

First work a sample of the edging with the suggested hook to make sure that your fabric is neat and even. If the stitches look loose and untidy as shown on the left, change to a smaller hook.
Similarly, if the stitches appear to be too tight so that the fabric is stiff and the stitches are difficult to work into, you should change to a larger hook.

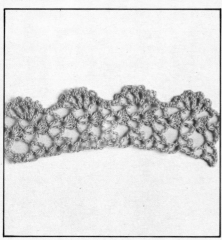

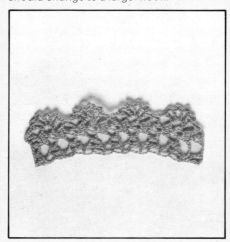

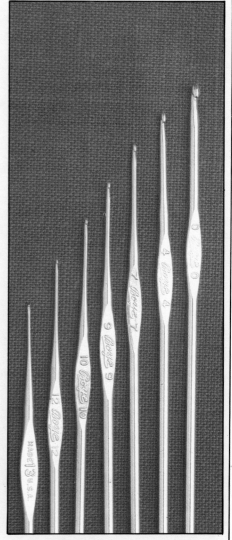

Fred Mancini

Washing and blocking

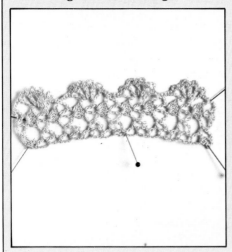

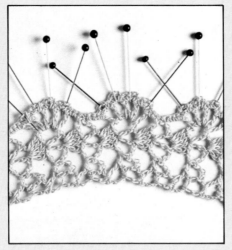

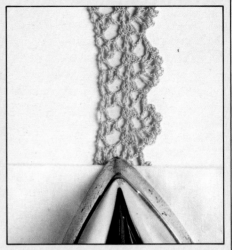

1 It is a good idea to wash and block the edgings *before* they are sewed onto the fabric to avoid any risk of shrinking. Use warm water and soap flakes rather than detergent to wash the edgings, and while they are still damp pin them out on a clean white cloth to the correct width and length, using rustproof tailor's pins. Take care not to stretch the straight edge of the fabric so that it remains completely flat.

2 Any circular motifs, petals or loops which have been worked on the lower edge of the fabric should be pinned separately. Make sure that each motif is the correct size and shape all the way along the edging.

3 Where a picot has been worked, pull this out so that it stands away from the main fabric. If necessary you could place a pin in the middle of each picot to hold it in place. When the edging is dry remove all the pins from the fabric and press *lightly* under a clean cloth with a hot iron if necessary.

Sewing the edgings onto your fabric

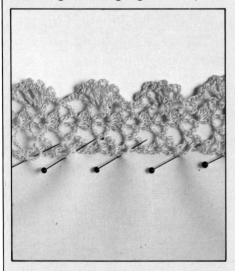

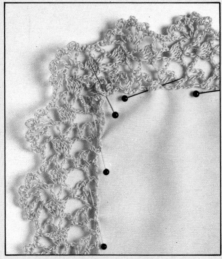

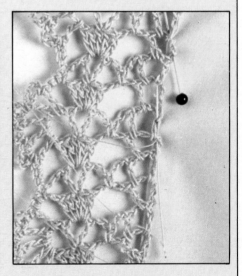

1 If fabric is unhemmed, turn under the raw edge to the wrong side, making a double hem in the normal way, and either machine-stitch or hand sew in place. With the right side of the crochet edging facing upward, pin the straight or top edge of the crochet to the right side of the fabric, as close to the edge as possible (as shown in the photograph) making sure that you do not stretch the edging while pinning it in place.

2 When pinning the crochet onto a square piece of fabric, ease the edging around each corner so that the lace is pinned evenly all around the material.

3 Use a fine needle and thread which matches the edging exactly. Overcast the edging to the fabric, working from right to left and making tiny diagonal stitches so that the sewing is invisible.

Lace-shell edging

The lace edging used to trim the sheet and pillowcase featured in this course is quite simple to work. Here we give you some useful hints to help you make the edging. Use them as a guide when following the row by row directions given on page 27. Once you have practiced this sample you should be able to work any of the edgings featured in the Stitch Wise section on page 26.

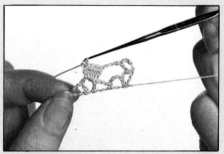

1 The pattern is worked over a small number of stitches. This means that you are working across the width of the edging rather than along the length of it, so that the length of the edging will be determined by the number of rows worked in all. Make sure that you place the hook under 2 loops in the foundation chain to ensure a firm edge.

2 On the 2nd row of the pattern 5 doubles are worked into the last loop or 2-chain space to create the first 5-double group or shell. This side of the fabric will become the bottom or lace edge of the crochet, so that there is no need to work a stitch into the turning chain in order to keep the edge straight as you would normally do when working crochet in rows.

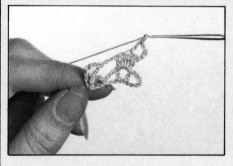

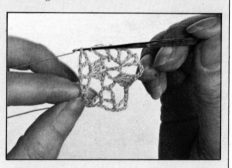

3 On the following row a series of doubles and chain loops are worked back along the row, incorporating the 5-double group into the pattern by working a double into the center of the double group. These 5-double shells or groups will lie horizontally across the fabric once the pattern has been completed, creating a firm lace pattern on which the circular motifs can be worked.

4 Begin to work the half circle or wheel motif at the end of the following row by working 5 doubles with a 2-chain space between each double all into the chain loop at the end of the row. By working a large group of stitches in this way at the edge of the fabric, you extend the circular motif beyond the edge, creating a lace effect.

5 To complete this row and hold the circular motif in shape, work a slip stitch into the middle of the 6 chains left unworked at the beginning of the base row so that in effect you are working down the side of the fabric, thus holding the motif in shape.

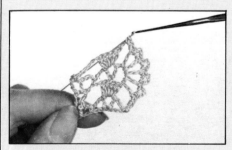

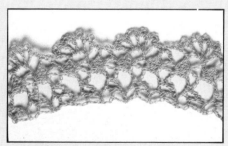

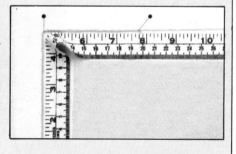

6 A 3-chain picot point is worked into each 2-chain space between the doubles to complete the motif. These stitches will now remain unworked on following rows.

7 Here is a sample of the completed edging in which a series of motifs have been worked consecutively to create the lace effect.

8 Some edging patterns are worked lengthwise, from the inner edge outward. You must begin by making a long length of chains. The pattern will specify the number of stitches in a repeat, but you must measure the fabric edge in order to calculate how many chains you will need. Where the edging is to be sewn around a corner, allow 1½in (4cm) extra for turning the corner.

Fred Mancini

Stitch Wise

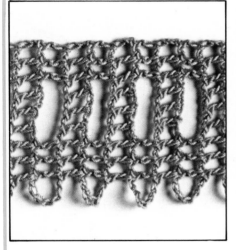

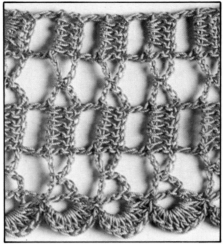

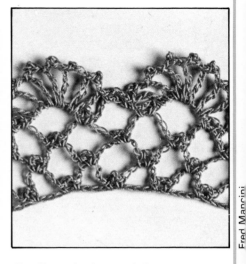

Fred Mancini

Trellis edging

Make 20 chains for the narrow end of the edging.
1st row 1dc into 6th ch from hook, *(1ch, skip next ch, 1dc into next ch) 7 times. Turn.
2nd row 7ch, 1dc into first dc at edge of work, (1ch, 1dc into next dc) twice, 7ch, skip next 3dc, (1dc into next dc, 1ch) twice, skip next ch, 1dc into next ch in turning chain. Turn.
3rd row 4ch, skip first dc, 1dc into next dc, 1ch, 1dc into next dc, (1ch, skip next ch, 1dc into next ch) 3 times, (1ch, 1dc into next dc) 3 times. Turn.
The 2nd and 3rd rows form the pattern and are repeated throughout.

Openwork edging

Make 25 chains for the narrow end of the edging.
1st row 1dc into 4th ch from hook, 1dc into each of next 4ch, 3ch, skip next 2ch, 1sc into next ch, 3ch, skip 2ch, 1dc into each of next 6ch, 3ch, skip 2ch, 1sc into next ch, 3ch, skip 2ch, work (1dc, 5ch, 1 sl st) all into last ch. Turn.
2nd row Work (1sc, 2hdc, 5dc) all into first 5ch loop, 1dc into first dc, 5ch, 1dc into next dc, 5ch, skip next 4dc, 1dc into next dc, 5ch, 1dc into next dc, 5ch, skip next 4dc, 1dc into top of turning chain. Turn.
3rd row 3ch, 4dc into first 5ch loop, 1dc into next dc, 3ch, 1sc into next 5ch loop, 3ch, 1dc into next dc, 4dc into next 5ch loop, 1dc into next dc, 3ch, 1sc into next 5ch loop, 3ch, 1dc into next dc, 5ch, 1 sl st into same place as last dc. Turn.
The 2nd and 3rd rows form pattern and are repeated throughout.

Scalloped-picot edging

This pattern is worked over a multiple of 12 chains plus 10.
1st row 1sc into 3rd ch from hook, 3ch, 1sc into next ch, *7ch, skip 4ch, 1sc into next ch, 3ch, 1sc into next ch, rep from * to end. Turn.
2nd row 10ch, *work (1sc, 3ch, 1sc) all into next 7ch loop, 7ch, rep from * to end, ending with 5ch, 1tr into last sc worked at beginning of previous row. Turn.
3rd row 1ch, (1sc, 3ch, 1sc) into first 5ch loop, *7ch, (1sc, 3ch, 1sc) into next 7ch loop, rep from * to end. Turn.
4th row As 2nd.
5th row 8ch, 1sc into 3rd ch from hook (picot), work (1tr, 3ch, 1sc into 3rd ch from hook) 5 times into next 7ch loop, 1tr into same loop, *(1sc, 3ch, 1sc) into next loop, (1tr and a 3-chain picot) 6 times into next loop, 1tr into same loop, rep from * to end.
Fasten off.

Extra edgings

Here are two alternative edgings that can be used to edge sheets and pillowcases or add a pretty border to a tablecloth.

Note If you want your edging to turn a corner you will need to allow an extra 1½in (4cm) for each corner.
These edgings have been worked in a fine mercerized crochet cotton, using a No. 7 (1.50mm) steel crochet hook.

Narrow green edging

Size
Width, 1in (2.5cm).

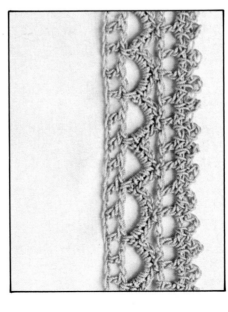

Make a ch the length required, having a multiple of 8 chains plus 4 extra.
Base row 1dc into 6th ch from hook, *1ch, skip 1ch, 1dc into next ch, rep from * to end. Turn.
1st row 1ch, 1sc into first dc, *5ch, skip next dc, 1sc into next dc, rep from * to end, finishing 5ch, skip last dc and next ch, 1sc into next ch of turning ch. Turn.
2nd row 1ch, 7sc into each 5ch loop. Turn.
3rd row 4ch, 1sc into 4th of 7sc, *3ch, 1sc into 4th of next 7sc, rep from * to end, finishing 1ch, 1dc into last sc. Turn.
4th row 4ch, *1dc into next sc, 1ch, 1dc into 2nd of next 3ch, 1ch, rep from * to end, finishing 1dc into next sc, 1ch, 1dc into 3rd of 4ch.
Turn.
5th row 1ch, (1sc, 3ch and 1sc) into each sp to end. Fasten off.

Bedside manner

This pretty, lacy edging will turn plain sheets and pillowcases into something special. The edging, worked in crochet cotton, is delicate and open.

Size
Width, 1½in (4cm).

Materials
150yd (137m) of a fine mercerized cotton makes approx. 2yd (2m) of edging
No. 7 (1.50mm) steel crochet hook

Make 14ch.
Base row 1dc into 7th ch from hook, 2ch, 1dc into next ch, 3ch, skip next 2ch, 1sc into next ch, 3ch, skip next 2ch, (1dc, 2ch and 1dc) into last ch. Turn.
1st row 5ch, 1dc into first 2ch sp, 3ch, 5dc into next 2ch sp. Turn.
2nd row 5ch, skip first 2dc, (1dc, 2ch and 1dc) into next dc, 3ch, 1sc into 2nd of next 3ch, 3ch, (1dc, 2ch and 1dc) into 3rd of 5ch. Turn.
3rd row 5ch, 1dc into first 2ch sp, 3ch, 5dc into next 2ch sp, 3ch, 1dc into 5ch loop, (2ch, 1dc) 4 times into same loop, 3ch, skip next row end, sl st into 3rd of 6ch at beg of base row. Turn.
4th row 1ch, 3sc into 3ch sp, (1sc, 3ch and 1sc) into each of next four 2ch sp, 3sc into next 3ch sp, 3ch, skip next 2dc, (1dc, 2ch and 1dc) into next dc, 3ch, 1sc into 2nd of 3ch, 3ch, (1dc, 2ch and 1dc) into 3rd of 5ch. Turn.
These 4 rows form the patt. Cont in patt for length required, noting that when working 3rd row, the last sl st is worked into sc before the 3ch sp of previous 4th row. Fasten off.

Victor Yuan

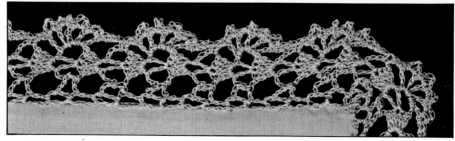

Wide green edging

Size
Width, 1⅜in (3.5cm).

To make
Make 13ch.
Base row 1dc into 6th ch from hook, 1ch, skip next 2ch, 2dc into next ch, 2ch, 2dc into next ch, 1ch, skip next 2ch, 1dc into last ch. Turn.
1st row 5ch, 1dc into 1ch sp, 1ch, (2dc, 2ch and 2dc) into 2ch sp — shell formed —, 1ch, 1dc into next 1ch sp. Turn.
2nd row As first row.
3rd row 5ch, 1dc into first 1ch sp, 1ch, work a shell into 2ch sp of shell, 1ch, 1dc into next sp, 3ch, do not turn, keeping the last loop of each on hook work 3dc into next 5ch loop on this edge, yo and draw through all loops on hook — called

3dc cluster or 3dc cl —, (3ch, 3dc cl) 3 times into same loop, 3ch, 1sc into next 5ch loop on this edge. Turn.
4th row 1ch, (1sc, 1hdc, 1dc, 1hdc and 1sc) into each of next five 3ch sp, 3ch, 1dc into next sp, 1ch, work a shell into

2ch sp of next shell, 1ch, 1dc into next 1ch sp.
Turn.
5th-8th rows As first row.
Rep rows 3 to 8 for length required, ending with a 4th row. Fasten off.

Ray Duns

Knitting / COURSE 34

Cleaning your knitting

Many yarns today are machine washable; the wrapper will indicate whether this is so. You will find that the yarn label usually gives detailed directions for cleaning and pressing and you should follow these instructions carefully. A yarn can be completely ruined by being washed or dried at a temperature that is not suitable for that particular fiber. And beware of dry cleaning, which is also not suitable for some types of synthetic fiber. Before beginning a piece of knitting it is a good idea to put one of the yarn labels with the cleaning instructions safely aside. Otherwise you may find upon completing your knitting that you have lost or thrown away all the wrappers. If the yarn does not give instructions on cleaning, it will at least indicate the fiber content and you could follow instructions on soap containers for the various types of fibers.

Remember that when the yarn is made of a mixed fiber—part natural and part synthetic—you should take into account what kind of care both of the fibers require. Then use the minimum temperature advised for washing, pressing and drying.

There are many soap powders and liquids available on the market for delicate fabrics. Read the labels and instructions thoroughly when choosing a soap suitable for your knitting. Some detergents contain bleach and should be avoided unless you are washing a pure cotton fiber that is white.

If you have the slightest doubt about whether your knitting can be machine-washed, it is always safest to wash the garment by hand. The lacy sweater on page 32 is a good example of a garment that must always be hand-washed; the nature of the yarn, mohair, and the texture of the garment, lacy openwork, require special treatment. The tennis sweater on page 30, however, is knitted in a man-made fiber that responds well to machine-washing; this is vital for sportswear, or for babies' and children's clothing that needs frequent laundering. Hand-knits on the whole need to be washed fairly frequently before they become heavily soiled; dirt can break the delicate fibers and spoil the appearance of the garment. What happens chemically is that the dirt turns into acid and forms an acid coating on the fibers. This coating will become thicker and more brittle with time. The reason freshly washed garments are so soft is that the hard acid coating has dissolved away with the washing.

If you have a heavily soiled piece of knitting that has been left for some time it is wise to try to remove some of the brittle coating on the fibers before washing. You can do this by preparing a bath of warm water with water softener in it. Immerse the garment in it and keep it submerged while moving it about for a few minutes. This will make the fabric more pliable and ready for the squeezing involved in the washing process.

Hand-washing and rinsing

When washing by hand use the quantity of soap which is recommended on the soap box or bottle. First dissolve the soap in a small amount of hot water, then add cold water until the correct temperature of around 104°F (40°C) is reached. This will not harm even the most delicate fiber. Before immersing the garment empty any pockets and turn the whole thing inside out. Then follow the step-by-step directions below for washing. Do not rush the rinsing process as any residue of soap left on the fabric is detrimental to it.

1 Submerge the garment in the suds. Work quickly, using your hands to expel soapy water by gently squeezing, never rubbing or wringing. Do not add more powder at this stage. Always support the garment with both hands when lifting it out of the water. Extra care is needed for bulky knits or open lacy patterns, the weight of the water can easily pull a garment out of shape.

2 Rinse the garment two or three times until the water is clear and all soapy deposits have disappeared. Remember to squeeze, not wring, and to support the wet garment. A fabric conditioner in the final rinse helps maintain the bulky, natural look of the yarn. But be sure to check the label on the fabric conditioner to ensure that it is suitable for the fiber you are washing.

3 Lift the garment out of the rinsing water, again supporting it with both hands. Squeeze to stop the dripping, then support the garment on a draining surface until you transfer it to a dryer or to a drying surface.

John Hutchinson

Drying

The nature and quality of the yarn dictates how you should spin and use clothes dryers. In most cases spinning gives the best results when you are just getting rid of moisture.

A light spin works for wool, especially large, bulky items, but you should never put a woolen garment in a tumble dryer, as the heat felts the fabric.

Synthetic fibers must be left until they are cold before giving them a short spin; if spun while still warm, they become distorted and creased. On the other hand, many synthetics can be put in the clothes dryer successfully.

The step-by-step photographs here show how to dry your woolens if tumble dryers are not available or advisable. The important thing to remember is that knitted garments must always be dried flat, never hung up. The weight of the water held in the yarn can easily distort the garment completely out of its original shape.

1 It is important to remove as much water as quickly as you possibly can. Do this by squeezing the garment gently between towels to prevent it from being pulled out of shape. Never resort to twisting and wringing the water out of the knitting. Prepare a flat surface—padded with newspaper and covered with a large, colorfast towel—for drying.

2 The garment should be inside out from washing: give it a shake to smooth out uneven stitches. Lay the damp garment on the drying surface and gently re-shape it back to its original size, smoothing out any wrinkles. Damp wool is very pliable and you can even make your garment slightly larger or smaller depending on whether you stretch it or smooth it into a smaller shape.

3 Use a tape measure to check that the original main measurements—around chest, length, sleeve seam—are correct. Smooth any ribbed edges in and fold them upwards to renew their elasticity.
Leave the garment until all the excess moisture has been absorbed by the towel and newspaper: never lift it until it is completely dry.

Care of knitted garments

Looking after your hand-knits makes sense when you consider the time and patience spent in producing them. One of the most common errors in storing knitted garments—one that can cause irreparable damage—is to hang them up. Ends of coat hangers or coat hooks make unsightly distortions of the fabric at the shoulders or back neck. Also, the elasticity of most knitted fabrics means that garments stretch downward when they are hung, especially if they are made in a bulky yarn.

1 When a garment is dry, it should not need pressing if it has been smoothed and flattened correctly during the drying process. However, if you think that pressing would improve it, first check with the original yarn label to choose the correct method.
Before storing a knitted sweater or jacket in a closed plastic bag on a shelf, fold the garment as shown in the pictures.

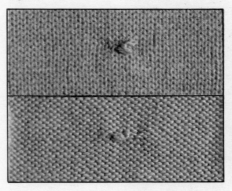

2 When wearing jewelry, you may "snag" a knitted fabric: it can catch in the yarn and pull a long, loose thread that hangs on the surface of the fabric. Never cut the loose thread off, or the fabric will unravel. Instead, push it through to the wrong side of the work using a blunt-ended yarn needle. Gently tighten the yarn until the stitch is the correct size, then knot the yarn to anchor the stitch.

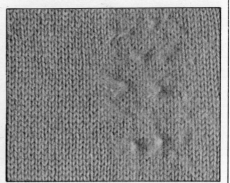

3 Everyday wear and tear of garments made from lightly-twisted yarns can cause "pilling." Small balls of yarn fluff up on the surface and spoil the appearance of the fabric. Gently pull off the balls of fluff, taking care not to snag the knitting. If the pilling is excessive, brush over the fabric lightly with a teasel or firm bristle brush to remove it.

Fred Mancini

Play the game!

This smart tennis sweater can be worn by a child for many other sports too.

Sizes

To fit 28[30:32:34:36]in (71[76:83:87:92]cm) chest.
Length, 19½[20½:21½:22¾:23¾]in (50[52:54:58:60]cm).
Sleeve seam, 16¼[16½:17:17:17¼]in (41[42:43:43:44]cm).
Note Directions for larger sizes are in brackets []; if there is only one set of figures it applies to all sizes.

Materials

10[10:11:12:13]oz (260[280:300: 320:360]g) of a sport yarn in main color (A)
1oz (20g) in each of 2 contrasting colors (B and C)
1 pair each Nos. 3 and 5 (3¼ and 4mm) needles; 1 cable needle (cn)

Gauge

22 sts to 4in (10cm) on No. 5 needles in stockinette st.

Back

*Using No. 3 (3¼mm) needles and A, cast on 93[99:103:109:115] sts.
1st row K1, *P1, K1, rep from * to end.
2nd row P1, *K1, P1, rep from * to end.
Rep these 2 rows once more. Join on B, with B K1 row, then rib 3 rows. With A K1 row, then rib 3 rows. Join on C, with C K1 row, then rib 3 rows. With A K1 row, then rib 3 rows. Cut off B and C. Change to No. 5 (4mm) needles. Beg patt.

1st row K19[21:22:23:25], P2, K6, P2, K35[37:39:43:45], P2, K6, P2, K to end.
2nd row P19[21:22:23:25], K2, P6, K2, P35[37:39:43:45], K2, P6, K2, P to end.
3rd row K19[21:22:23:25], P2, sl next 3 sts onto cn and leave at back of work, K3, then K the sts from cn—called Cable 6 or C6, P2, K35[37:39:43:45], P2, C6, P2, K to end.
4th row As 2nd row.
5th-8th rows Work first and 2nd rows twice.
These 8 rows form patt.*
Cont in patt until work measures 12½[13:13½:14½:15]in (32[33:34:37:38]cm) from beg; end with WS row.

Shape armholes

Keeping patt correct, bind off 7[8:8:8:9] sts at beg of next 2 rows.
Next row K1, sl1, K1, psso, patt to last 3 sts, K2 tog, K1.
Next row Patt to end.
Rep last 2 rows until 63[67:71:75:79] sts rem. Cont straight until work measures 7[7½:8:8¼:8¾]in (18[19:20:21:22]cm) from beg of armhole; end with WS row.

Shape shoulders

Bind off 6[6:7:7:8] sts at beg of next 4 rows and 6[7:7:8:8] sts at beg of foll 2 rows. Cut off yarn and leave rem 27[29:29:31:31] sts on a holder.

Front

Work as for back from * to *. Cont in patt

until work measures 10¼[11:11½:12:13]in (26[28:29:30:33]cm) from beg; end with WS row.

Divide for neck

Next row Patt 43[46:48:51:54], K2 tog, K1, turn, leave rem sts on spare needle. Finish this side first. Patt 3 rows.
Next row Patt to last 3 sts, K2 tog, K1.
Dec one st at neck edge on every foll 4th row, *at same time* when work measures same as back to armhole, ending at side edge, shape armhole:
Next row Bind off 7[8:8:8:9] sts, patt to end.
Next row Patt to end.
Next row K1, sl1, P1, psso, patt to end.
**Cont to dec in this way, dec one st at armhole edge on next and 6[6:6:7:7] foll alternate rows and at neck edge as before. Keeping armhole straight, cont to dec at neck edge until 18[19:21:22:24] sts rem. Cont straight until front is same length as back to shoulder; end at armhole edge.

Shape shoulder

Bind off 6[6:7:7:8] sts at beg of next and foll alternate row. Work 1 row. Bind off.**
Return to sts on spare needle. With RS facing place next st on safety pin, join yarn to next st, K1, sl 1, K1, psso, patt to end. Patt 3 rows.
Next row K1, sl 1, K1, psso, patt to end.
Dec one st at neck edge on every foll 4th row, *at same time* when work measures same as back to armhole, ending at side edge, shape armhole:

Gary Warren

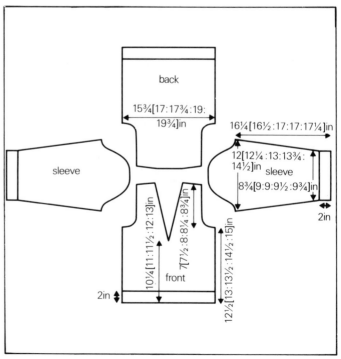

back

15¾[17:17¾:19: 19¾]in

16¼[16½:17:17:17¼]in

sleeve

12[12¼:13:13¾: 14½]in sleeve
8¾[9:9:9½:9¾]in

2in

10¼[11:11½:12:13]in

7[7½:8:8¼:8¾]in

front

12½[13:13½:14½:15]in

2in

Brian Mayor

Next row Bind off 7[8:8:8:9] sts, patt to end.

Next row Patt to last 3 sts, K2 tog, K1. Complete to match first side of neck, working from ** to **.

Sleeves

Using No. 3 (3¼mm) needles and A, cast on 48[50:50:52:54] sts.

Rib row *K1, P1, rep from * to end. Rep last row 3 times more. Join on B, with B K1 row, then rib 3 rows. With A K1 row then rib 3 rows. Join on C, with C K1 row, then rib 3 rows. With A K1 row, then rib 3 rows. Cut off B and C. Change to No. 5 (4mm) needles. Beg patt.

1st row K19[20:20:21:22], P2, K6, P2, K to end.

2nd row P19[20:20:21:22], K2, P6, K2, P to end.

3rd row K19[20:20:21:22], P2, C6, P2, K to end.

4th row As 2nd row.

5th–8th rows Work first and 2nd rows twice.

These 8 rows form patt. Cont in patt, working extra sts in stockinette st inc one st at each end of next and every foll 9th[9th:8th:7th:7th] row until there are 66[68:72:76:80] sts. Cont straight until work measures 16¼[16½:17:17:17¼]in (41[42:43:43:44]cm) from beg; end with WS row.

Shape top

Bind off 7[8:8:8:9] sts at beg of next 2 rows. Dec one st at each end of next and every foll 4th row until 36[34:38:44:46] sts rem, then one st at each end of every alternate row until 24[24:26:28:28] sts rem. Now dec one st at each end of every row until 18[18:20:22:22] sts rem. Bind off.

Neckband

Join right shoulder seam. With RS facing, using No. 3 (3¼mm) needles and A, pick up and K 62[66:68:72:74] sts along left front neck, K st from safety pin and mark it with colored thread, pick up and K 62[66:68:72:74] sts along right front then K back sts from holder inc in last st. 153[163:167:177:181] sts.

1st row (WS) Work in K1, P1 ribbing to within 2 sts of marked st, sl 1, K1, psso, P1, K2 tog, rib to end. Join on B.

Next row With B, K to within 2 sts of marked st, sl 1, K1, psso, K1, K2 tog, K to end.

Next row With B, rib to within 2 sts of marked st, sl 1, psso, P1, K2 tog, rib to end.

Next row With A, K to within 2 sts of marked st, sl 1, K1, psso, K1, K2 tog, K to end.

Next row With A, rib to within 2 sts of marked st, sl 1, K1, psso, P1, K2 tog, rib to end. Join on C.

Next row With C, K to within 2 sts of marked st, sl 1, K1, psso, K1, K2 tog, K to end.

Next row With C, rib to within 2 sts of marked st, sl 1, K1, psso, P1, K2 tog, rib to end.

Next row With A, K to within 2 sts of marked st, sl 1, K1, psso, K1, K2 tog, K to end.

Next row With A, rib to within 2 sts of marked st, sl 1, K1, psso, P1, K2 tog, rib to end. With A, bind off in ribbing, dec as before.

To finish

Press or block according to yarn used. Join left shoulder and neckband. Set in sleeves then join side and sleeve seams.

Gary Warren

Soft and lacy

For those who like the shapely look . . . make this lacy patterned sweater in a soft fluffy yarn.

Sizes

To fit approx 32[36:40]in (83[92:102]cm) bust.
Length, 24½[25½:26½]in (62[64:66]cm).
Sleeve seam, 17½in (44cm).
Note Directions for larger sizes are in brackets []; if there is only one set of figures it applies to all sizes.

Materials

14[15:16]oz (375[400:425]g) of medium-weight mohair yarn
1 pair each Nos. 7 and 9 (5 and 6mm) knitting needles
Set of four No. 7 (5mm) double-pointed needles or a circular needle

Gauge

14 sts and 20 rows to 4in (10cm) in patt on No. 9 (6mm) needles.

Back

Using No. 7 (5mm) needles cast on 59[67:75] sts.
1st row K1, *P1, K1, rep from * to end.
2nd row P1, *K1, P1, rep from * to end.
Rep these 2 rows for 1½in (4cm); end with 2nd row. Change to No. 9 (6mm) needles.
Beg patt.
1st row (RS) K1, *yo, sl 1, K1, psso, K6, rep from * to last 2 sts, yo, sl 1, K1, psso.
2nd and every alternate row P to end.
3rd row K2, *yo, sl 1, K1, psso, K3, K2 tog, yo, K1, rep from * to last st, K1.
5th row K3, *yo, sl 1, K1, psso, K1, K2 tog, yo, K3, rep from * to end.
7th row K1, K2 tog, yo, *K5, yo, sl 2, K1, p2sso, yo, rep from * to last 8 sts, K5, yo, sl 1, K1, psso, K1.
9th row K5, *yo, sl 1, K1, psso, K6, rep from * ending with K4 instead of K6.

11th row K3, *K2 tog, yo, K1, yo, sl 1, K1, psso, K3, rep from * to end.
13th row K2, *K2 tog, yo, K3, yo, sl 1, K1, psso, K1, rep from * to last st, K1.
15th row K4, *yo, sl 2, K1, p2sso, yo, K5, rep from * ending with K4.
16th row As 2nd.
These 16 rows form patt. Rep them 4 times more.
Shape raglan armholes
**1st row K1, sl 1, K1, psso, patt to last 3 sts, K2 tog, K1.
2nd row P to end.**
Rep last 2 rows until 23[27:31] sts rem; end with P row. Leave sts on holder.

Front

Work as for back.

Sleeves

Using No. 7 (5mm) needles cast on 29[29:33] sts. Rib 1½in (4cm) as for back; end with 2nd row and inc 22[22:18] sts evenly across last row. 51 sts. Change to No. 9 (6mm) needles. Rep 16 patt rows as for back 5 times in all.
Shape raglan
Rep from ** to ** as for back armhole shaping until 15[11:7] sts rem; end with

P row. Leave sts on holder.

Neckband

Join raglan seams. Using set of No. 7 (5mm) needles or circular needle and with RS facing, K across all sts on holders, K2 tog at each seam. 72 sts. Work 1½in (4cm) in rounds of K1, P1 ribbing. Bind off in ribbing.

Belt

Using No. 7 (5mm) needles cast on 9 sts for center back edge. Work ¾[1¼:1½]in (2[3:4]cm) K1, P1 ribbing as for back. Cont in ribbing inc one st at each end of next and every foll 7th row until there are 17 sts. Work 3¼[3½:4]in (8[9:10]cm) straight. Dec one st at each end of next and every foll 7th row until 9 sts rem. Cont straight until work measures 19[19¾:20½]in (48[50:52]cm) from beg. Inc one st at each end of next and every foll 7th row until there are 17 sts.
Bind off.
Work another piece in the same way.

To finish

Do not press. Join side and sleeve seams. Join center back seam on belt.

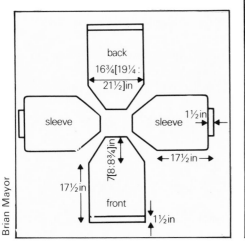

back
16¾[19¼:21½]in

sleeve   sleeve   1½in

17½in   ←17½in→

7[8:8¾]in

17½in   front   1½in

Brian Mayor

Gary Warren

Knitting/COURSE 35

More lace knitting and patterns

Lace patterns are usually a combination of decorative increasing and decreasing (see Knitting course 22, Volume 5, page 47): decreased stitches are compensated with increased ones, made in such a way that holes form in the fabric.

Most lacy knitting looks best worked in fine yarns which normally require fine needles. However, larger needles make a more effective, looser fabric that looks lacier—this is because the holes don't close up.

To test a lacy stitch for an article of your own design, you will need to make a stitch gauge sample with the yarn and needles you intend to use. For the sample cast on approximately enough stitches for a 4in (10cm) width. Work until the sample is square, then block and press gently before measuring the gauge.

The step-by-step sequences here depict two unusual, but simple, lacy fabrics involving other knitting techniques that you already know—decreasing by lifting one stitch over others to work open star stitch, and a mixture of bobble and long, dropped stitches for hyacinth stitch.

Hyacinth stitch

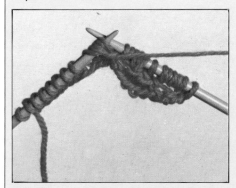

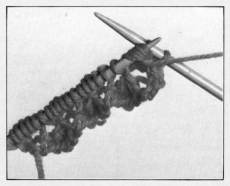

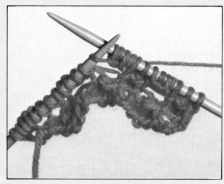

1 Cast on a multiple of 6 stitches plus 3 extra. Purl the first row, then work the 2nd row, K1, make 5 sts out of 1 by (K1, P1, K1, P1, K1) all into next st—see Knitting course 25, Volume 6, page 39—K5 tog, rep from * to last 2 sts, make 5 sts out of next 1, K1.

2 Purl the 3rd row, then work the 4th row. Start as follows: K1, *K5 tog.

3 Next, make 5 sts out of next 1, rep from * to last 6 sts, K5 tog, K1. Purl the 5th row.

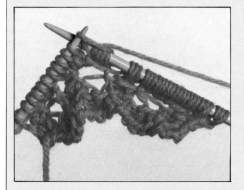

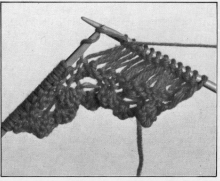

4 Prepare long stitches on the 6th row: K to end, but wind yarn 3 times around right-hand needle—instead of once—for each st.

5 To complete the first pattern repeat work the 7th row P to end, dropping the extra loops made by winding yarn 3 times around needle in previous row (these loops make long stitches).

6 Repeat the 2nd to 7th rows until the pattern is the depth you require. The fabric is an unusual combination of bobbles and long, dropped stitches formed in a very lacy flower shape.

Fred Mancini

Open star stitch

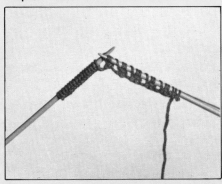 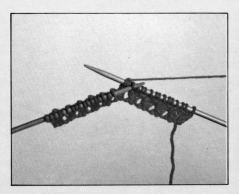 

1 Cast on a multiple of 3 stitches. To work the first row (RS) K2, *yo, K3 then use the left-hand needle point to lift first of these sts over the other 2 and off the right-hand needle, rep from * to last st, K1. Purl all WS rows.

2 Now work the 3rd row K1, *K3, using the same technique as in the first row lift the first of these sts over the other 2, yo, rep from * to last 2 sts, K2. Purl the next row.

3 Repeat these 4 rows until the fabric is the depth you require. The "yo" in pattern rows makes a hole while the extra stitch is compensated for by lifting a stitch over two others. This decreased stitch forms a distinctive bar on the right side of the pattern.

Making a ribbon-rosette trimming

The successful appearance of a garment often depends on the care taken with assembling and professional finishing touches such as trimmings. A christening cape (see opposite page) is a once-in-a-lifetime garment and deserves special attention. You could buy a fabric flower and sew it on but, when the rest of the garment is handmade, it's much more appropriate to make your own flower trimmings.

These step-by-step pictures show how to make a simple, but effective, rosette, about 2½in (6cm) in diameter. You can vary the diameter by using wider ribbon, or alter the density of the petals by using a longer length. Use nylon or satin ribbon for the best flower formation and add a different-colored bead for the center.

1 Here a 23in (58cm) length of 1in (2.5cm) wide ribbon makes a rosette about 2½in (6cm) across. Using a sewing needle and matching thread (here it is contrast-colored for clarity), secure at one end and make small running stitches close to edge along two short sides and one long side of ribbon.

2 Don't fasten off when the running stitches are complete. Pull the end of thread to gather the stitches, pushing the gathers tightly together at the left-hand end of the ribbon. The ribbon automatically tends to twist at this stage.

3 Beginning at the left-hand end of the ribbon, coil it around in a circle so that the gathered edge is always in the center.

4 Fold the coiled ribbon tightly together, gripping the top and lower center between the fingers of your left hand. Take the needle through the center to the lower edge.

5 Working from the back of the flower, overcast all the layers of gathers tightly together at the center, leaving a long end for sewing the rosette on the garment. Arrange the ribbon petals into an attractive shape and add a pearly button.

Fred Mancini

For a special baby's special day

This delicate lacy cape, knitted in a sport yarn, makes an ideal wrap for a baby on his or her christening day.

Sizes
Length to back neck, 24½in (62cm).
Width around lower edge, 42in (108cm).

Materials
9oz (250g) of a sport yarn
1 pair each Nos. 2 and 3 (3 and 3¼mm) knitting needles
1 each Nos. 4 and 5 (3¾ and 4mm) circular needles, 30in (75cm) long
Size B (2.50mm) crochet hook
Ribbon to make 2 rosettes

Gauge
21 sts to 3½in (9cm) in patt using No. 5 (4mm) needles.

Cape
Using No. 4 (3¾mm) circular needle cast on 253 sts for lower edge. Working backward and forward in rows, work 8 rows garter st. Change to No. 5 (4mm) circular needle. Beg patt.
1st and every foll alternate row (WS) K6, P to last 6 sts, K6.
2nd row K6, K2 tog, *yo, K3, yo, K into front and back of next st, yo, K3, yo, sl 1, K2 tog, psso, rep from * ending last rep sl 1, K1, psso instead of sl 1, K2 tog, psso, K6.

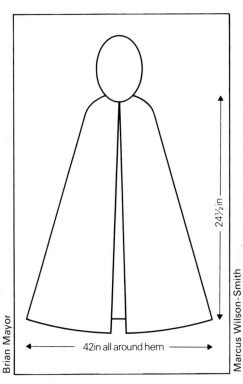

42in all around hem

24½in

Brian Mayor

Marcus Wilson-Smith

4th row K6, sl 1, K1, psso, *yo, sl 2, K1, p2sso, yo, K2 tog, yo, sl 1, K1, psso, (yo, sl 2, K1, p2sso) twice, rep from * ending last rep K2 tog instead of second sl 2, K1, p2sso, K6.

6th row K8, *K2 tog, yo, K3, yo, sl 1, K1, psso, K3, rep from * to last 8 sts, K8.

8th row K7, *K2 tog, yo, K1 tbl, yo, sl 1, K2 tog, psso, yo, K1 tbl, yo, sl 1, K1, psso, K1, rep from * to last 6 sts, K6. These 8 rows form patt. Cont in patt until work measures 22in (56cm); end with first row. Change to No. 3 (3¼mm) needles.

Next row K20, (K2 tog, K1, K2 tog, K2) 30 times, K2 tog, K21. 192 sts. Work 9 rows garter st.

Shape yoke

1st row K6, *K1, K2 tog, rep from * to last 6 sts, K6. 132 sts. Work 13 rows garter st.

15th row As first. 92 sts. Work 7 rows garter st.

23rd row K7, *K2 tog, K1, rep from * to last 7 sts, K7. 66 sts.

24th row K to last 11 sts, turn.

25th row Sl 1, K to last 11 sts, turn.

26th row Sl 1, K to last 18 sts, turn.

27th row As 26th.

28th row Sl 1, K across sts to end. Work 5 rows garter st.
Bind off loosely.

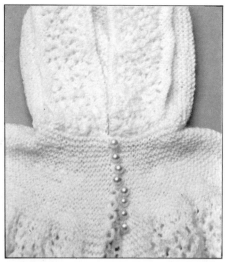

Gary Warren

Hood

Using No. 2 (3mm) needles cast on 101 sts. Work 4 rows garter st. Change to No. 3 (3¼mm) needles. Work 17 rows patt as for cape, omitting 6 sts in garter st at each end of every row and dec one st at each end of last row. 99 sts. Cont in garter st until work measures 8in (20cm) from beg.

Shape crown

1st row *K7, K2 tog, rep from * to end. 88 sts.

2nd and every foll alternate row K to end.

3rd row *K6, K2 tog, rep from * to end. 77 sts.

5th row *K5, K2 tog, rep from * to end. 66 sts.

Cont in this way, working one st less between dec on every alternate row, until 11 sts rem. Cut off yarn, thread through rem sts, gather and fasten off securely.

To finish

Join back seam of hood from crown to beg of shaping. Fold patt section of hood to RS and slip stitch in position. Easing hood to fit neck, sew to cape. Using crochet hook work 8 button loops down garter st yoke. Sew on buttons. Make 2 rosettes with ribbon and stitch one to each side of cape at lower edge.

Stitch Wise

Lace diamond pattern

This pattern has the same multiple of stitches as that used in the baby's christening cape (see page 35).
Cast on a multiple of 10 sts plus 1 extra.

1st and every alternate row (WS) P to end.

2nd row K2, *K2 tog, (K1, yo) twice, K1, sl 1, K1, psso, K3, rep from * ending last rep K2.

4th row K1, *K2 tog, K1, yo, K3, yo, K1, sl 1, K1, psso, K1, rep from * to end.

6th row K2 tog, *K1, yo, K5, yo, K1, sl 1, K2 tog, psso, rep from * ending last rep sl 1, K1, psso instead of sl 1, K2 tog, psso.

8th row K1, *yo, K1, sl 1, K1, psso, K3, K2 tog, K1, yo, K1, rep from * to end.

10th row K2, *yo, K1, sl 1, K1, psso, K1, K2 tog, K1, yo, K3, rep from * ending last rep K2.

12th row K3, *yo, K1, sl 1, K2 tog, psso, K1, yo, K5, rep from * ending last rep K3. These 12 rows form the patt.

Chevron-pointed lace

This is another alternative for the cape.
Cast on a multiple of 10 sts plus 1 extra.

1st and every alternate row (WS) P to end.

2nd row K1, *yo, sl 1, K1, psso, K2 tog, yo, K1, rep from * to end.

4th row K2, *yo, sl 1, K1, psso, K3, K2 tog, yo, K3, rep from * ending with K2.

6th row K3, *yo, sl 1, K1, psso, K1, K2 tog, yo, K5, rep from * ending with K3.

8th row K4, *yo, sl 1, K2 tog, psso, yo, K7, rep from * ending with K4.

10th, 12th and 14th rows K1, *sl 1, K1, psso, K2, yo, K1, yo, K2, K2 tog, K1, rep from * to end.

These 14 rows form the patt.

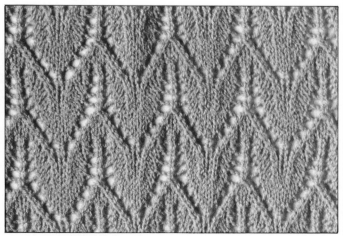

Knitting / COURSE 36

Finishing off and sewing on a lacy edging

An edging usually has one straight edge—for attaching it to the main fabric—while the opposite edge can be scalloped, indented, wavy or pointed.

The width of the edging is set by the number of cast-on stitches and can be narrow, medium or wide; the length depends on the number of rows worked. Cotton thread is the traditional material for edgings. It can be starched and blocked to hold its shape and show off the open lacy patterns to their best effect. But you can use other kinds of yarn if you prefer.

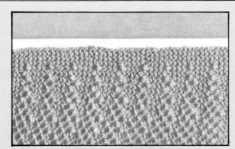

1 Work the edging—this is the table cloth edging on page 39—until the straight top edge fits all around the outer edge of the item to which it is to be attached.

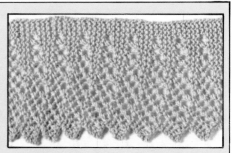

2 To see the true effect of the lacy pattern, block the edging so that the holes open out. Keep the top edge straight at the original measurement while stretching the pattern open toward the lower edge.

3 Join the cast-on and bound-off edges if necessary. Check whether the fabric to be edged is already hemmed and turn up a small hem if necessary. Lay the edging in position on the right side of the hemmed edge, about ⅛in (3mm) in, and pin it in place.

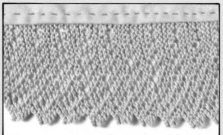

4 It is best to sew the edging on by hand: sometimes machine stitching may be recommended, but this could stretch the knitting. Using sewing thread matching the edging, stab stitch (see Knitting course 18, Volume 4, page 50) the edging in place. This picture shows how the work looks on the wrong side.

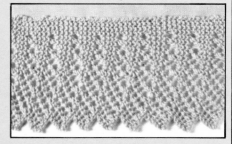

5 Here the edging has been sewn in place: the stab stitches are indistinguishable against the knitted background. It is advisable to remove edging when you wash the object. Launder the edging separately, then re-block it before sewing it back on.

Making a lacy bias edging

Some edgings are specifically designed to fit all the way around a curved edge such as a skirt hem, a cuff, or the outer edge of a circular mat. These are called bias edgings and when laid on a flat surface form a curve. A bias edging is meant to be joined at the ends to form a ring. The two ends fit together, with pattern matching, to make a diagonal seam. The directions here are for a pretty, lacy bias edging that has a variety of uses. This edging includes a technique commonly used for forming indented patterns at the edge—binding off groups of stitches.

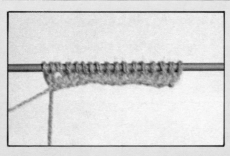

1 Cast on 15 stitches. Purl one row. Work the first row: (RS) Sl1, K1, (yo, K2 tog) 3 times, (K1, yo) twice, K1, K2 tog, yo twice, K2 tog.

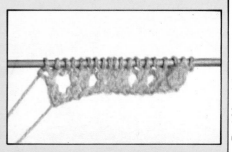

2 Work the 2nd row: K2, P13, K2 and 3rd row; Sl1, K1, (yo, K2 tog) 3 times, K1, yo, K2, yo, K1, K2 tog, yo twice, K2 tog, K1. You can see that the lacy pattern is beginning to appear.

continued

Fred Mancini

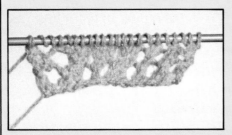

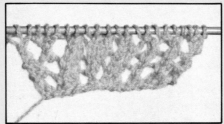

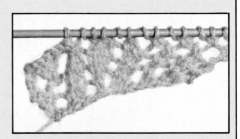

3 Continue with the 4th row: K3, P14, K2 and 5th row: Sl 1, K1, (yo, K2 tog) 3 times, K1, yo, K3, yo, K1, K2 tog, (yo, K2 tog) twice. Note that you are increasing stitches at the left-hand end of this needle—the lower edge of the work.

4 Work the 6th row: K2, P1, K2, P15, K2 and 7th row: Sl 1, (K1, yo) twice, (sl 1, K1, psso, yo) twice, K2 tog, yo, (K2 tog) twice, yo, K3 tog, K6. The holes made by winding yarn around needle (yo twice) are extra large—see them at the left-hand edge of the work.

5 Complete the pattern repeat, and shape scallop at lower edge by binding off stitches, by working the 8th row: bind off 6 sts knitwise, P next 12 sts on left-hand needle, K2. Here we show the wrong side of the work.

6 Repeat the 8 pattern rows until the straight edge fits around the curved edge that you want to sew it onto, ending with an 8th row. Bind off. This edging has such a strong bias effect that the straight top edge naturally lies in a gentle curve.

7 Block the edging, maintaining the natural curve. Form the edging into a circle and join the cast-on and bound-off edges, matching the pattern lines exactly. The join slopes because it is a bias fabric.

8 Place the edging in position with garter stitch border just overlapping fabric that it is being sewed onto: it can hang down and decorate a cuff or skirt hem or lie flat around the edge of a circular mat. Sew in place.

Stitch Wise

Scalloped-wave edging

This is a narrow edging with a subtle scalloped edge. The number of stitches increases and decreases to form peaks. Cast on 13 sts.
1st and every other row K2, P to last 2 sts, K2.
2nd row Sl 1, K3, yo, K5, yo, K2 tog, yo, K2.
4th row Sl 1, K4, sl 1, K2 tog, psso, K2, (yo, K2 tog) twice, K1.
6th row Sl 1, K3, sl 1, K1, psso, K2, (yo, K2 tog) twice, K1.
8th row Sl 1, K2, sl 1, K1, psso, K2, (yo, K2 tog) twice, K1.
10th row Sl 1, K1, sl 1, K1, psso, K2, (yo,

K2 tog) twice, K1.
12th row K1, sl 1, K1, psso, K2, yo, K1, yo, K2 tog, yo, K2.
14th row Sl 1, (K3, yo) twice, K2 tog, yo, K2.
Rep these 14 rows for length needed.

Vine edging

Picot points are featured around the graceful scallops of this medium-depth edging. Insert a pin into each single loop at the edge when you wash and pin it out; this draws the loop away from the next stitch and emphasizes the picot. Cast on 20 sts and K1 row.
1st row K3, yo, P2 tog, K3, yo, K10, yo, P2 tog.

P2 tog.
2nd row Yo, P2 tog, K14, yo, P2 tog, K3.
3rd row K3, yo, P2 tog, K3, yo, K1, yo, K10, yo, P2 tog.
4th row Yo, P2 tog, K16, yo, P2 tog, K3.
5th row K3, yo, P2 tog, K3, (yo, K1) 3 times, yo, K10, yo, P2 tog.
6th row Yo, P2 tog, K20, yo, P2 tog, K3.
7th row K3, yo, P2 tog, K6, yo, K1, yo, K13, yo, P2 tog.
8th row Yo, P2 tog, K22, yo, P2 tog, K3.
9th row K3, yo, P2 tog, K13, then using point of right-hand needle (lift 2nd st on left-hand needle over first and off needle) 9 times, yo, P2 tog.
10th row Yo, P2 tog, K13, yo, P2 tog, K3.
Rep these 10 rows for the length needed.

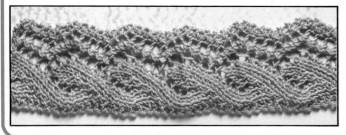

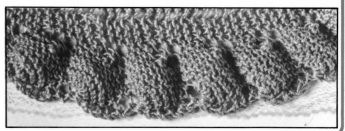

Lace for your linen

This lace edging will add a delicate, decorative touch to any plain tablecloth. Make enough to go around the edge and attach it with stab stitch.

Sizes
Width at widest point, 3in (7.5cm).

Materials
1 x 95yd (87m) of a fine pearl cotton makes approx 1yd (1m) of edging
1 pair of No. 00 (2mm) knitting needles

Gauge
16 sts and 25 rows to 2in (5cm) in patt worked on No. 00 (2mm) needles.

Edging
Using No. 00 (2mm) needles cast on 20 sts. K1 row. Beg patt.
1st row K4, (yo, K2 tog) 7 times, yo, K2.
2nd and every other alt row K to end.
3rd row K7, (yo, K2 tog) 6 times, yo, K2.
5th row K10, (yo, K2 tog) 5 times, yo, K2.
7th row K13, (yo, K2 tog) 4 times, yo, K2.
9th row K to end.
10th row Bind off 4 sts, K to end. 20 sts.
These 10 rows form patt.
Rep them for length required, ending with a 9th row.
Bind off.

*Traditional and alternative Shetland shawl formations
*Grafting
*Casting on with a separate length of yarn
*Patterns for Shetland shawls

Traditional Shetland shawl formation

Shetland shawls are world famous for their lacy patterns and gossamer-fine quality. Traditionally the yarn had to be so fine—often 1 ply—that the finished shawl could be pulled through a wedding ring. Originally these shawls had neither cast-on nor bound-off edges, as such harsh lines would detract from the cobwebby effect. They were built up from one corner of the outer lace border. The finished shawls were washed, then "dressed" by lacing them to special frames to stretch the lace patterns to their best advantage. The step-by-step directions for making the shawls shows how to do this in a contemporary setting. Modern shawls are usually made in thicker Shetland yarn and are often constructed by alternative, less painstaking methods. These shawls are remarkably soft and elastic, making them extremely useful for wrapping up a baby, putting around the shoulders of an elderly person or invalid, or as high fashion wear.

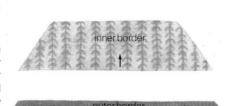

1 Begin knitting the shawl at one corner of the outer border as indicated by the arrow: the outer border is worked sideways for the lengths of one side of the shawl. For the deep inner border, pick up stitches (sometimes 200 to 300) along the straight edge of the outer border. Again work in the direction of the arrow, decreasing stitches at either side to form mitered corners.

2 The division between the inner border and center is marked with a row of holes made by working "yo, K2 tog." Work the center in garter stitch, making sure that it is square by knitting as many horizontal ridges (formed by two rows) as there are stitches. After completing the center, leave the stitches on the needle.

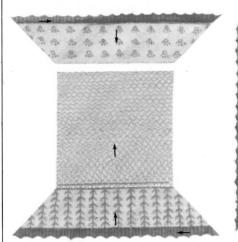

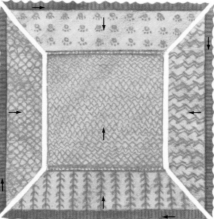

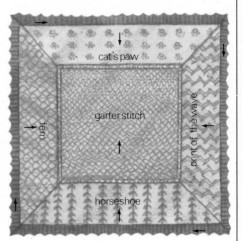

3 Make a second outer and inner border as before. Join the border to the main section by a form of grafting that produces holes similar to the opposite edge: thread the yarn alternately through two stitches from the center and two from the border. When joining always keep the center of the shawl on top and the border behind it.

4 Make a third outer and inner border. Pick up stitches (corresponding in number to those in the border) along the side edge of the shawl center. Graft the center and border stitches together as explained. Complete the fourth side in the same way.

5 Only the four corners remain to be joined: pick up the same numbers of stitches from each side of the join on separate needles. Graft the stitches together by taking one stitch from one needle and one from the other in a herringbone movement.

Alternative method of joining

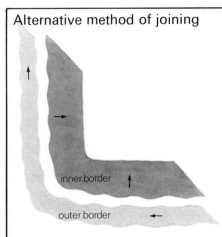 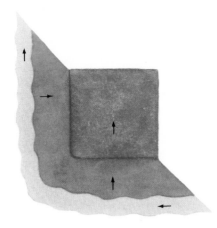 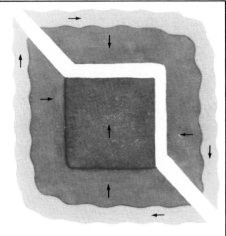

inner border

outer border

Terry Evans

1 The first stage is similar to the traditional method: knit the outer border sideways to fit around **two** sides of the shawl. This outer border will be a long straight strip. Pick up stitches along the straight edge of the outer border and work the inner border, decreasing stitches to form corner shaping. A circular needle—used to knit in rows—is a great help in coping with the large number of stitches.

2 Work the center in garter stitch directly onto one side of the border section. Knit the first row to the middle of the border section (first side of the center), then pick up one stitch from the remaining border edge (second side of center). Turn work and knit two stitches together, then knit to end of row. Continue in this way, picking up stitches along edge, until center is square. Bind off loosely.

3 Work another outer and inner border to fit around the remaining two sides of the center. Bind off very loosely at the end of the inner border. Join border to center and sew up corners, keeping stitching loose to allow for stretching.

Grafting

Grafting is a method of joining two knitted fabrics horizontally so that the seam is invisible. The normal method of binding off gives a hard, rigid edge which is not always suitable for some designs; shoulder seams, toes of socks and neckbands are frequently grafted. Lacy fabrics,

such as the border and center of a Shetland shawl, are also often grafted together so that the seam does not detract from the light, open patterns. The loops of the two fabrics to be joined —these may both be bound-off edges or a bound-off and cast-on edge (see Casting

on with a separate length of yarn, page 42)—must be the same in number and laid one behind the other. The join is made with a tapestry needle and yarn, entering each stitch twice in a certain pattern, according to the fabric, and pulling the stitches together.

Grafting two edges together on a stockinette stitch fabric

Fred Mancini

1 The two pieces to be joined must have the same number of stitches: the knit side is on the outside of both pieces. At the end of the front section, cut off the yarn leaving a long end—about three times the length to be joined. Place the needles, with points facing to the right, together in your left hand.

2 Thread the long end of yarn (here a contrasting color has been joined on for clarity) into a large tapestry needle. Insert the needle knitwise (as if to knit) through first stitch on back needle and draw yarn through, but leave the stitch on the needle.

3 Then insert needle knitwise through first stitch on front needle and draw yarn through; slip this stitch off front needle.

continued

4 Insert needle purlwise through next stitch on front needle: draw yarn through, but leave stitch on needle. Insert needle purlwise through first stitch on back needle; draw yarn through and slip stitch off back needle. Insert needle knitwise through next stitch on back needle; leave stitch on needle.

5 Repeat steps 3 and 4 until all the stitches have been eliminated from the needles. Note that the needle and yarn must pass twice through each stitch before slipping it from the knitting needle. Constantly check the tightness of the grafting to make sure it matches the rest of your work.

6 Here is the nearly completed joining being worked with matching yarn. As long as the work is neat and the tightness correct, it is impossible to detect the seam—it merely looks like an ordinary row of knitting, even on the back of the fabric.

Grafting two edges together on a garter stitch fabric

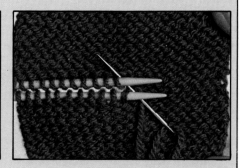

1 The two needles with the stitches to be grafted must be one behind the other with the needle points at the right; there must be the same number of stitches on each needle. The ridge made by the last row of knitting must be on the outside of the front needle and inside of the back needle. Leave a long end of yarn on the front piece as you will need to use it when grafting the knitting.

2 Follow steps 2, 3 and 4 of grafting a stockinette stitch fabric, but insert the needle purlwise in step 2; then knitwise in step 3; and then purlwise, then knitwise and purlwise in step 4. Work until all the stitches have been eliminated from the needles.

3 This is how the finished joining looks when it is worked correctly with matching yarn: the only sign of a seam is a slightly wider space between ridges. You must tighten the stitches carefully and neatly as you work to prevent too big a gap.

Casting on with a separate length of yarn

In lace knitting it is preferable to avoid hard lines of casting on wherever possible, as they detract from the delicate fabric. It is possible to produce a loose edge using large needles and a special method of casting on with a separate length of yarn. If the fabric has to be joined at any stage—say it is the center of a Shetland shawl and requires a knitted border—the contrasting cast-on row can be unraveled so that the loops of the main fabric can be grafted to another edge to make an undetectable seam.

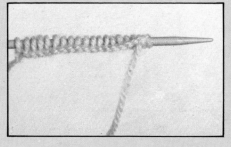

1 Using a pair of needles two sizes larger than those used for the main fabric and the two-needle method of casting on, take an extra length of yarn in the same quality—but a contrasting color—and cast on the required number of stitches.

2 Change to the correct size needles and the yarn for the main fabric. Continue in stockinette stitch or pattern following the pattern directions as usual.

Fred Mancini

3 When the main fabric is finished and you need to graft the cast-on and another edge together, you must undo the length of contrasting yarn to expose the loops of the main fabric. Begin with the right side of the work facing you and unravel the stitches as follows.

4 Use the end of a knitting needle or a large tapestry needle to gently undo each stitch in the cast-on row individually, following the direction of the yarn so that it doesn't knot. Hold the unraveled stitches on a correct-sized knitting needle inserted from the right-hand edge into the knit side of each stitch.

5 When the cast-on row is completely undone, check that there are the original number of stitches held on the needle. You may need to transfer the stitches to another needle by simply slipping them knitwise so that the knit side of the work is in the correct position for grafting. Notice that the bound-off stitches now form the lower edge.

Shetland magic

Once you have mastered the technique, these stunning Shetland shawls will be easy to knit.

Serge Krouglikoff

Sizes
Both shawls are approximately 39in (100cm) square.

Materials
Sport yarn
Shawl with striped border *6oz (150g) in main color (A)*
3oz (75g) in contrasting color (B)
2oz (50g) each of contrasting colors (C and D)
1 pair long No. 5 (4mm) knitting needles or circular needle
Plain-colored shawl *12oz (325g)*
1 pair No. 5 (4mm) needles

Gauge
Shawl with striped border 23 sts and 40 rows to 4in (10cm) in garter st on No. 5 (4mm) needles.
Plain-colored shawl 22 sts and 30 rows to 4in (10cm) in stockinette st on No. 5 (4mm) needles.

Shawl with striped border

Outer border
Using No. 5 (4mm) needles and B, cast on 12 sts.
1st row K12.
2nd row K10, yo, K2.
3rd row Yo, K2 tog, K11.
4th row K9, yo, K2 tog, yo, K2.
5th row and every alternate row Yo, K2 tog, K to end.
6th row K8, (yo, K2 tog) twice, yo, K2.
8th row K7, (yo, K2 tog) 3 times, yo, K2.
10th row K6, (yo, K2 tog) 4 times, yo, K2.
12th row K5, (yo, K2 tog) 5 times, yo, K2.
14th row K5, (K2 tog, yo) 5 times, K2 tog, K1.
16th row K6, (K2 tog, yo) 4 times, K2 tog, K1.
18th row K7, (K2 tog, yo) 3 times, K2 tog, K1.
20th row K8, (K2 tog, yo) twice, K2 tog, K1.
22nd row K9, K2 tog, yo, K2 tog, K1.
24th row K10, K2 tog, K1.
25th row As 5th.
Rep the 2nd-25th rows 22 times more, then the 2nd-24th rows again.
Next row Bind off 12, do not break off yarn, but turn and pick up and K 288 sts along the straight edge of work. 289 sts.

Inner border
Join in A.
1st row *K1, (K2 tog) 4 times, (yo, K1) 7 times, yo, (K2 tog) 4 times, rep from * 11 times more, K1. K 5 rows.
7th row As first.
K 1 row. Change to C and K 4 rows.
13th row *K1, (K2 tog) 4 times, (yo, K1) 6 times, yo, (K3 tog) 3 times, patt 96 as first row, K1, (K3 tog) 3 times, (yo, K1) 6 times, yo, (K2 tog) 4 times, rep from * once more, K1. K 3 rows.

Change to A and K 2 rows.
19th row *K1, (K2 tog) 3 times, (yo, K1) 6 times, yo, K2 tog, (K3 tog) twice, patt 96 as first row, K1, (K3 tog) twice, K2 tog, (yo, K1) 6 times, yo, (K2 tog) 3 times, rep from * once more, K1.
K 5 rows. Change to D.
25th row *K1, (K2 tog) 3 times, (yo, K1) 5 times, yo, K2 tog, (K3 tog) twice, patt 96 as first row, K1, (K3 tog) twice, K2 tog, (yo, K1) 5 times, yo, (K2 tog) 3 times, rep from * once more, K1.
K 5 rows.
31st row *K1, (K2 tog) 3 times, (yo, K1) 5 times, yo, (K2 tog) 3 times, patt 96 as first row, K1, (K2 tog) 3 times, (yo, K1) 5 times, yo, (K2 tog) 3 times, rep from * once more, K1. K 1 row.
Change to A and K 4 rows.
37th row *K1, (K2 tog) 3 times, (yo, K1) 4 times, yo, (K2 tog) twice, K3 tog, patt 96 at first row, K1, K3 tog, (K2 tog) twice, (yo, K1) 4 times, yo, (K2 tog) 3 times, rep from * once more, K1.
K 3 rows. Change to B and K 2 rows.
43rd row *K1, (K2 tog) twice, K3 tog, (yo, K1) 4 times, yo, (K2 tog) twice, patt 96 as first row, K1, (K2 tog) twice, (yo, K1) 4 times, yo, K3 tog, (K2 tog) twice, rep from * once more, K1. K 5 rows. Change to A.
49th row *K1, (K2 tog) 3 times, (yo, K1) 3 times, yo, K2 tog, K3 tog, patt 96 as first row, K1, K3 tog, K2 tog, (yo, K1) 3 times, yo, (K2 tog) 3 times, rep from * once more, K1.
K 5 rows.
55th row * K1, (K2 tog) twice, (yo, K1)

3 times, yo, K3 tog, K2 tog, patt 96 as first row, K1, (K2 tog) twice, (yo, K1) 3 times, yo, K3 tog, K2 tog, rep from * once more, K1.
K 1 row. Change to C and K 4 rows.
61st row * K1, K2 tog, K3 tog, (yo, K1) twice, yo, (K2 tog) twice, patt 96 as first row, K1, (K2 tog) twice, (yo, K1) twice, yo, K3 tog, K2 tog, rep from * once more, K1.
K 3 rows. Change to A and K 2 rows.
67th row *K1, (K2 tog) twice, yo, K1, yo, (K2 tog) twice, patt 96 as first row, K1, (K2 tog) twice, yo, K1, yo, (K2 tog) twice, rep from * once more, K1.
K 5 rows. Change to D.
73rd row *K1, (K2 tog) twice, yo, K3 tog, patt 96 as first row, K1, K3 tog, yo, (K2 tog) twice, rep from * once more, K1.
K 5 rows.
79th row K1, (K3 tog) twice, (yo, K2 tog) 48 times, yo, K3 tog, K1, K3 tog, (yo, K2 tog) 48 times, yo, (K3 tog) twice, K1.
K 1 row. Cut off all colors except A.
Cont throughout in A.

Center
Next row K102, turn.
Next row K2 tog, K to end.
Rep these 2 rows until all sts have been worked in. Bind off LOOSELY.
Work the outer border and inner border again, binding off LOOSELY after the 80th row.

To finish
Sew the straight edge of the second border to the two sides of the center square. Join the corners of the borders. Dampen shawl, spread out and pin to correct shape and size then leave to dry.

Plain-colored shawl

Center

Using No. 5 (4mm) needles and the 2-needle method, cast on 140 sts. Beg with a K row, work about 190 rows stockinette st (or until work is square); end with P row.

Next row K1, K twice into each of next 9 sts, K to last 11 sts, K twice into each of next 10 sts, K1. 159 sts.

Next row P to end.

Border pattern

1st row K1, *K3, yo, K2 tog, K1, rep from * to last 3 sts, K3.

2nd row P to end.

3rd row K1, *K2 tog, yo, K1, yo, K2 tog, rep from * to last 2 sts, K2.

4th row P to end.

5th row K1, K2 tog, *yo, K3, yo, K3 tog, rep from * to last 6 sts, yo, K3, yo, K2 tog, K1.

6th row P to end.

Rep these 6 rows 8 times more.

Next row (K1, K twice into next st) 6 times, K to last 13 sts, (K1, K twice into next st) 6 times, K1.

Next row P to end, turn and cast on 12 sts for edging.

Edge pattern

1st row K11, K next st tog with first st of border. Turn.

2nd row K2, P2, K1, P5, yo, K2.

3rd row K2, (K1, P1) into next st, K1, yo, K3, yo, K3 tog, yo, K2 tog, K next st tog with next st of border. Turn.

4th row K2, P8, K4.

5th row K5, yo, K6, yo, K2 tog, K next st tog with next st of border. Turn.

6th row K2, P9, yo, K2 tog, yo, K2.

7th row K2, (K1, P1) into next st, K1,

(K1, P1) into next st, K1, yo, K1, K2 tog, P1, K2 tog, K1, yo, K2 tog, K next st tog with next st of border. Turn.

8th row K2, P3, K1, P4, K7.

9th row Bind off 5 then K next 2 sts, yo, K1, yo, K2 tog, P1, K2 tog, yo, K2 tog, K next st tog with next st of border. Turn. 12 sts.

Rep 2nd-9th rows until all sts are worked off; end with RS row.

Leave the edge sts on the needle, using the same needle pick up and K 29 sts down the edge of the border toward the center. Cut off yarn.

Using a spare needle and with WS row of work facing and the border just worked on the left, pick up and P 135 sts along the edge of the center, working toward the needle with the sts on (but not across these sts). Turn.

Next row K1, K twice into each of next 12 sts, K to last 13 sts, K twice into each of next 12 sts, K to last 13 sts, K twice into each of next 12 sts, K1.

Next row P to last st, then P last st tog with first of border that was left. Turn. Always working the last st of P rows tog

with next st of border, work 6 patt rows of border 9 times; end with P row.

Next row (K1, K twice into next st) 6 times, K to last 13 sts, (K1, K twice into next st) 6 times, K1.

Next row P back to edge sts left on needle, P last st tog with first st of edge.

Cont in edge patt as on first side until all border sts have been worked.

Work along third side as for second side, pick up 29 sts along edge of border. Cut off yarn and turn.

With WS of work facing, skip first 12 cast-on sts, pick up and P 29 sts down edge of border, then 135 sts along edge of center. Turn.

Work as for other borders, but on every row work last st tog with first st of border. After 9 patts have been completed, work edging as before, binding off rem 12 sts at end.

To finish

Sew 12 bound-off sts to the 12 cast-on sts at beg of first edge. Dampen shawl, spread out and pin to correct shape and size, then leave to dry.

* Making fitting adjustments to knitting patterns
* Making style adjustments to knitting patterns
* Knitting a fringe
* Patterns for fringed jackets

Making style adjustments to knitting patterns

When you find a knitting pattern that you like, first check your own measurements against the ones given in the pattern. They are usually listed under the heading "sizes" and include the main ones required—for example, for a sweater they would be bust or chest size and lengths of garment and sleeve. In Stitch by Stitch patterns, information about the size of the garment piece is given in a measurement diagram: if a sweater is to fit a 32in (92cm) bust and the back and front are each 17½in (44cm) across, then there is 2¼in (6cm) of ease around the bust. Fitting adjustments must be limited at this stage to amending lengths, any alterations to the width of a piece of knitting usually necessitate redesigning that section, which is a much more complicated task. Work out modifications in advance by reading the pattern thoroughly before starting. Remember that alterations may affect the amount of yarn needed.

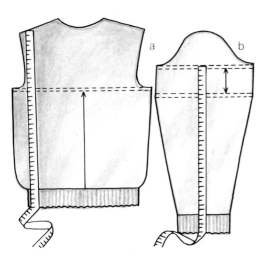

The most common adjustment is the lengthening or shortening of a sweater. Check the finished length, usually measured from the outer shoulder edge to the hem, and then add or subtract any extra length in the main body before the underarm shaping is reached (**a**).
Beware of altering a garment that has a complicated stitch pattern involving a large repeat.
The sleeve length on the garment is measured from under the arm to the lower edge of the cuff down a central vertical line of stitches. Add or subtract length in the rows of straight knitting (about 1½in [4cm]) which follow the sleeve shaping but precede the shaping of the sleeve top (**b**).
The last pattern row at the underarm must be the same as that on the back and front at the same point so that the pattern matches across the back and front and sleeve top.

Skirts may be knitted downward from the waist or upward from the hem. Those that are knitted downward often require continuous shaping and, by measuring the garment against yourself, you can stop at any length you like. With skirts that are knitted upward it is necessary to lengthen or shorten them in the straight section that often precedes the shaping (**c**): in this case it is vital to do the calculations before you begin knitting.

Making fitting adjustments to knitting patterns

While looking at knitting patterns you may frequently come across designs that are almost suitable but that you'd like to change in some way—substituting another stitch pattern, or a round for a V-neck, or turning a cardigan into a pullover.
There are a few possibilities and a great many pitfalls in coping with such style changes unless you are a very experienced knitter. Some of the most common adjustments are discussed here: feasible solutions are suggested wherever possible, otherwise the reasons for avoiding certain style changes are given. Once again it is important to remember that any changes usually affect the quantity of yarn you need.

Making a sleeveless pullover or vest from a pullover or cardigan pattern is quite easy to manage. Choose a V-neck sweater or cardigan design (a sleeveless garment with a high round neckline looks rather odd) and simply disregard the sleeve instructions (**d, e**). It is then essential to finish the armholes, usually with a ribbed band to match the waistband and neckband. The garment may have shaped armholes (for set-in sleeves) or a dropped shoulder line with straight edges (for an unshaped sleeve top). In either case, join the shoulder seams and leave the side seams open, then pick up stitches for the ribbed band around the armhole using the same yarn and needles as those used for the waistband.

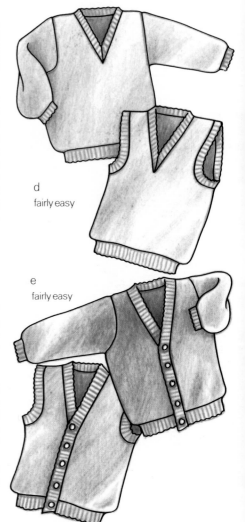

d
fairly easy

e
fairly easy

Making a different style neckline is quite complicated unless you have expert knowledge of knitting design. Of course, it is possible to make a V-neck instead of a round one or vice versa, but it is a design problem and requires advance calculations (**f**). Future knitting courses will deal with designing knitting.

You can at this stage easily change a round neckband by extending it into a turtleneck, or vice versa, and the basic neckline stays the same in either case (**g**).

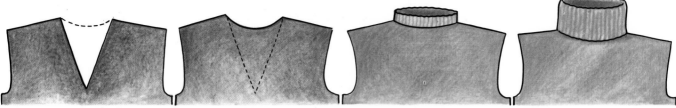

f requires expert knowledge

g easy

Changing the look of the fabric with stripes and stitch patterns is an effective way of restyling (**h**). If the original garment is in stockinette stitch, you can adapt it in a number of different ways without any complicated calculations.

The simplest method of all is to use the reverse side of the fabric as the right side to give it a more textured appearance. Stripes are also an easy way of livening up a garment; these may be regular or irregular stripes on a stockinette stitch background or broken stripes in reverse stockinette stitch. You can also add color-work borders or patterns as long as you are careful with the stitch gauge where the yarns not in use are carried across the back of the work.

h fairly easy

Changing the stitch pattern should be approached with caution, no matter how much you like the shape and design of the original garment (**i**). First make a stitch gauge sample of the stitch you want to substitute using the recommended yarn and needles. Compare it with the gauge stated in the pattern—you will probably find it is different. Even if there is a small difference which cannot be corrected by a change of needles, this can massively distort the overall proportions of sections of the garment.

Unless you are lucky enough to find a stitch pattern that knits up to the same size as the original, then it is better to leave this type of adjustment until you are very experienced.

i requires expert knowledge

Terry Evans

Knitting a fringe

The most widely used fringing in knitting consists of strands of yarn threaded through an edge in individual tufts and then knotted together. The fringe shown here is knitted separately.

The total number of stitches needed combines those for a border and those for the looped fringe (which is initially knitted and then unraveled); the stitches in both sections may vary according to how deep you want them to be. When the fringe stitches are unraveled the loops are about two and a half times longer than the original knitted fringe section and you should bear this in mind when planning.

Try knitting fringes in different types of yarn—thick and luxurious ones for heavy draperies or a bedspread, or fine glittery ones for evening clothes.

1 Cast on a number of stitches for the border and the fringe: here it is 9 stitches (4 for the border and 5 for the fringe). Work in garter stitch until the border fits along the edge to be fringed.

2 Bind off one less stitch than the total number of border stitches—in this case 3. Cut the yarn from the main ball and draw it through the last border stitch (the loop on the right-hand needle) to fasten it off.

3 Slip the remaining 5 stitches off the left-hand needle. Start to unravel the loops, beginning at the lower edge and working upward: unravel the first stitch in the first ridge, then pull the yarn gently to undo consecutive stitches.

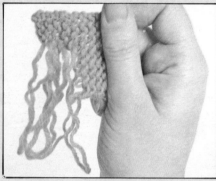

4 Don't worry when the 5 fringe stitches are unraveled—it is impossible to unravel any of the border stitches. Undo each ridge individually until all the fringe stitches are free, including the cast-on edge at the right-hand side.

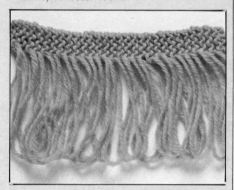

5 This is the finished fringe with the vertical garter stitch border at the top edge and a long, looped fringe formed by the unraveled rows of knitting.

6 You may want a cut fringe instead of a looped one. If you don't mind the fringe being slightly shorter, simply trim neatly across the lower edge. If the fringe must remain the same length, insert the scissors through a number of loops at a time, extend them gently and cut through.

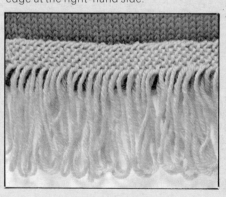

7a The fringe may be sewn onto the edge of a fabric—such as the bottom of a skirt—so that it hangs down. Position the straight edge of the border about 2in (5cm) in from the edge of the fabric and stab stitch the border in place.

7b There is no need for the fringe to hang from an edge; it could be positioned anywhere on the background (see the fringed jackets opposite). To sew the fringe on in this case, turn it upside down so that the straight edge is level with the line you are trimming. Slip stitch the straight edge in position, then fold the fringe over so that it hangs in the correct direction.

Cowboy style

These bright-colored jackets are great for the outdoor life. There's one for every member of the family.

Sizes

To fit 28[30:32:34:36:38:40:42]in (71[76:83:87:92:97:102:107]cm) chest/bust.

Length, 20[21½:22½:23½:24½:25½:26: 26½]in (51[55:57:60:62:65:66:67]cm).

Sleeve seam, 16[16½:17:17½:17½:18:19: 19]in (41[42:43:45:45:46:48:48]cm).

Note Directions for larger sizes are in brackets []; where there is only one set of figures it applies to all sizes.

Materials

Knitting worsted
Jacket A 8[9:9:10:10:11:11:12] x
  1oz (25g) balls in yellow
8[8:9:9:11:11:12:12] balls in green
3[3:4:4:5:5:6:6] balls in blue
2 balls in red
Jacket B 12[13:13:14:14:15:15:16] x
  1oz (25g) balls in green
4[5:5:5:6:6:6:6] balls each in
  yellow and red

Jacket C 11[12:12:13:14:14:15:15]
  x 1oz (25g) balls in blue
9[9:9:10:11:11:11:12] balls in red
1 pair each Nos. 2 and 4 (3 and
  3¾mm) knitting needles
7[7:7:8:8:8:8] buttons; holder

Gauge

24 sts and 32 rows to 4in (10cm) in stockinette st on No. 4 (3¾mm) needles.

Note

These directions are for a plain-colored jacket: if you want a multi-colored one, (A, B or C), refer to the appropriate diagram and change colors accordingly.

Back

Using No. 2 (3mm) needles cast on 80 [86:92:98:104:110:116:122] sts. Work 2¼in (6cm) K1, P1 ribbing.
Next row Rib 0[3:1:4:2:0:3:1], *K twice into next st, rib 7[7:8:8:9:10:10:11], rep from * to last 0[3:1:4:2:0:3:1] sts, rib to end. 90[96:102:108:114:120:126:132] sts.
Change to No. 4 (3¾mm) needles. Beg with K row, cont in stockinette st until work measures 12½[13½:14:14½:15:15½:15½:15½]in (32[34:36:37:38:39:39:39]cm) from beg; end with P row.

Shape raglan

Bind off 3 sts at beg of next 2 rows.
Next row K1, sl 1, K1, psso, K to last 3sts, K2 tog, K1.
Next row K1, P to last st, K1.
Rep last 2 rows once more. Change to seed st patt for yoke – K1 (P1, K1) to end. Cont to shape raglan on next and foll alternate rows until 26[28:30:32:34:36:38:40] sts rem. Bind off.

Right front

Using No. 4 (3¾mm) needles cast on 24[24:26:26:28:28:30:30] sts for pocket lining. Beg with a K row, work 26[26:28:28:30:30:32:32] rows stockinette st. Cut off yarn and leave these sts on a holder.
Using No. 2 (3mm) needles cast on 38[40:44:46:50:52:56:58] sts. Work 2¼in (6cm) K1, P1 ribbing.
Next row Rib 1[2:2:3:2:1:3:4], *K twice into next st, rib 6[6:7:7:8:9:9:9], rep from * to last 2[3:2:3:3:1:3:4] sts, K twice into next st, rib to end. 44[46:50:52:56:58:62:64] sts.
Change to No. 4 (3¾mm) needles. Beg with a K row, work 26[26:28:28:30:30:32:32] rows stockinette st.

Divide for pocket

Next row K10[11:12:13:14:15:16:17] sts, sl next 24[24:26:26:28:28:30:30] sts onto holder for pocket top, K the sts of pocket lining, K to end.
Cont in stockinette st until front measures same as back to underarm; end at side.

Shape raglan

Bind off 3 sts at beg of next row.
Next row K to last 3 sts, K2 tog, K1.
Next row K1, P to end.
Rep last 2 rows once more. Change to seed st patt for yoke. Cont to shape raglan on next and foll alternate rows until 20[20:23:23:26:26:29:29] sts rem, ending with a WS row.

Shape neck

Cont to dec one st at raglan edge, bind off 2 sts at beg of next row, then dec one st at neck edge until 6 sts rem.

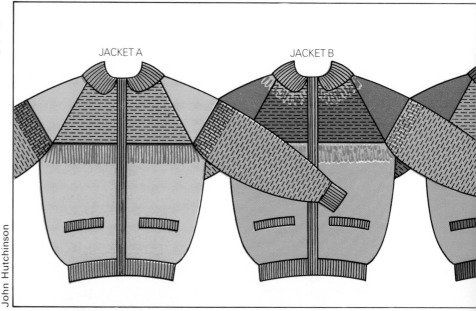

JACKET A   JACKET B

John Hutchinson

Gary Warren

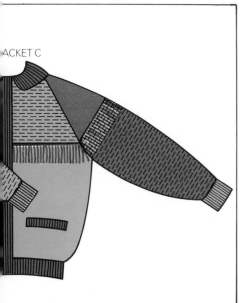

ACKET C

Cont to shape raglan edge only until 2 sts rem. K2 tog. Fasten off.

Left front

Work to match right front, reversing shaping and working "K1, sl 1, K1, psso" instead of "K2 tog, K1" for raglan shaping.

Sleeves

Using No. 2 (3mm) needles cast on 42 [46:46:50:50:54:54:58] sts. Work 2[2:2:2:2:3:3:3]in (6[6:6:6:6:8:8:8]cm) K1, P1 ribbing. Change to No. 4 (3¾mm) needles. Cont in seed st, inc one st at each end of next and every foll 6th row until there are 70[76:80:84:88:94:98:102] sts. Cont straight until work measures 16 [16½:17:17½:17½:18:19:19]in (41[42: 43:45:45:46:48:48]cm) from beg; end with WS row.

Shape raglan

Bind off 3 sts at beg of next 2 rows.

Next row K1, sl 1, K1, psso, patt to last 3 sts, K2 tog, K1.
Next row K1, patt to last st, K1.
Rep last 2 rows once more. Beg with a K row, change to stockinette st for yoke. Cont to shape raglan on next and foll alternate rows until 6[8:8:8:8:10:10:10] sts rem; end with P row. Bind off.

Button band

Using No. 2 (3mm) needles cast on 8[8:8:8:8:10:10:10] sts. Work in K1, P1 ribbing until band, slightly stretched, fits up front edge. Bind off in ribbing.

Buttonhole band

Using No. 2 (3mm) needles cast on 8[8: 8:8:8:10:10:10] sts. Work 4 rows K1, P1 ribbing.
1st buttonhole row Rib 3[3:3:3:3:4:4:4] sts, bind off 2 sts, rib to end.
2nd buttonhole row Rib to end, casting on 2 sts over those bound off in last row. Cont in rib, making 6[6:6:6:7:7:7:7] more buttonholes at intervals of 2¾[2¾:3¼:3½:3:3¼:3¼:3¼]in (7[7:8:9: 7.5:8:8:8]cm) measured from base of last one, until band, slightly stretched, fits up front edge. Bind off in ribbing.

Pocket tops

With RS facing and using No. 2 (3mm) needles, rejoin yarn to 24[24:26:26: 28:28:30:30] pocket top sts left on holder. Work 6[6:6:6:6:8:8:8] rows K1, P1 ribbing. Bind off in ribbing.

Collar

Using No. 2 (3mm) needles cast on 157 [161:165:169:173:177:181:185] sts. Work 4 rows K1, P1 ribbing.
Next row Rib 5, sl 1, K2 tog, psso, rib to last 8 sts, K3 tog, K5.
Rib 3 rows. Rep last 4 rows until 137[141:145:149:153:157:161:165] sts rem. Bind off 10 sts firmly at beg of next 10 rows. Bind off rem sts.

Fringe border

Using No. 4 (3¾mm) needles cast on 7 sts. Work in garter st until strip is required length. At beg of last row bind off 3 sts for border fastening off the 3rd st firmly (4 sts rem on left-hand needle). Sl sts off needle and unravel each ridge as far as 3st border to make one loop of fringing each time.

To finish

Press with a warm iron over a damp cloth. Join raglan, then side and sleeve seams. Sew down pocket linings on WS. Sew button and buttonhole bands in position. Matching center back, sew bound-off edge of collar to neck edge. Sew on buttons to correspond with buttonholes. Sew fringe border in place on top of yoke edge and around collar if desired. Looped ends of fringe may be cut and trimmed.

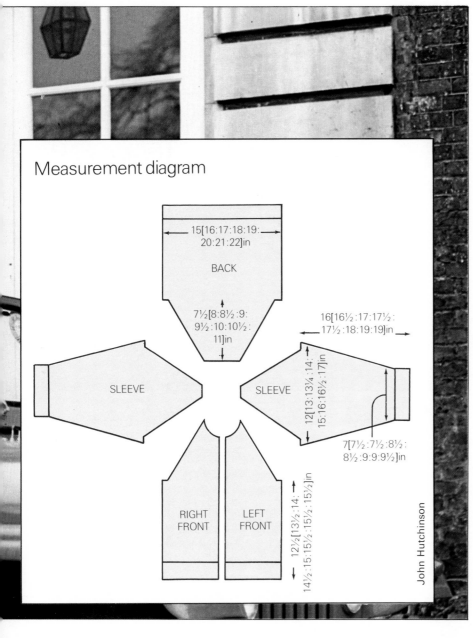

Measurement diagram

15[16:17:18:19: 20:21:22]in

BACK

7½[8:8½:9: 9½:10:10½: 11]in

16[16½:17:17½: 17½:18:19:19]in

SLEEVE

SLEEVE

12[13:13¾:14: 15:16:16½:17]in

7[7½:7½:8½: 8½:9:9:9½]in

RIGHT FRONT

LEFT FRONT

12½[13½:14: 15:16:16½:15½]in

14½:15:15½:15½:15½]in

John Hutchinson

Shoestring

Jolly juggler

Brighten a pair of overalls with this clever little juggling clown worked in cross-stitch.

Ron Kelly

John Hutchinson

Finished size
The motif measures 5¼in (13.5cm) tall and 3¾in (9.5cm) wide, but can be reduced or enlarged as described below.

Materials
A pair of children's overalls
1 skein each of stranded embroidery floss in red, white, black, yellow and green
Piece of Penelope (double thread) canvas 6in (15cm) square with 10 pairs of threads to 1in (2.5cm)
No. 21 or 22 tapestry needle
Hard pencil or canvas marker
Sewing needle and thread

1 Find the center of the bib by measuring up from the top of the waistband and across from the side of the bib and basting along these two lines.
2 Find the center of the canvas by measuring vertically and horizontally, and mark a cross where center pairs of threads intersect. (Be sure to mark the pairs of threads and not spaces between pairs.)
3 Place the canvas over the bib with the centers matching. Check that the upper and lower edges of the canvas are equidistant from, and parallel to, the upper edge of the bib and the top of the waistband. Pin and baste the canvas in place around the edges.

4 Using 6 strands of red floss in the tapestry needle, embroider the mouth, placing the center stitch over the vertical center pair of threads and the second horizontal pair above the center, as shown.
5 Work the rest of the design following the chart and using 6 strands of floss throughout.
6 When the embroidery is completed, saturate it with warm water. Gently pull out the canvas threads.
7 Press the work on the wrong side.
To adjust the size of the motif use smaller or larger gauge canvas and fewer or more strands of thread.

Sewing / COURSE 33

*Cording seams
*Binding center front and
 sleeve openings
*Shirt with scarf:
 adapting the pattern
 directions for making

Cording seams

Cording is formed by covering a cord with a bias strip of fabric. It is then enclosed between the two layers of a seam so that a slightly ridged strip of fabric is visible on the right side of the garment.

Cording can be used to finish the faced edge of a garment, such as the front lapel edges of a jacket and around pockets or cuffs, or it can be used as a decorative detail to emphasize seaming. The cording can be made either to match the garment fabric or to contrast with it so that it forms an obvious detail.

If the garment fabric is very sheer, it is advisable to line the piping strip with a bias strip of matching lining fabric or plain cotton which will prevent the cord from showing through on the right side when the cording is finished.

The narrowest filler cords are usually used on clothing, but knitting yarn can be substituted on sheer or very soft fabrics, where a more delicate cording is needed.

1 Measure the seam to be corded and cut a bias strip this length (see Volume 1, page 56).
The width of the strip should be $1\frac{1}{4}$in (3cm) plus three times the diameter of the cord or yarn. This allows $\frac{5}{8}$in (1.5cm) seam allowances once the cord is inserted.

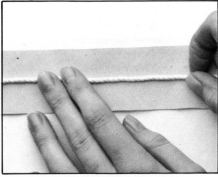

2 Place the cord on the center of the wrong side of the strip.

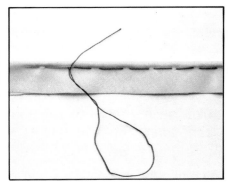

3 Fold the bias strip in half with the wrong sides together, and, keeping the raw edges together, baste close to the cord.

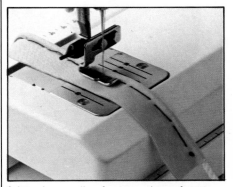

4 Attach a cording foot or a zipper foot to the machine and adjust the stitch length so that it is slightly longer than usual. Sew as close as possible to the cord or yarn.

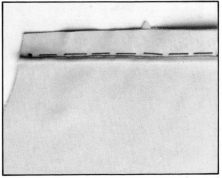

5 Baste the covered cord to the main section of the garment with a seam to be corded. For example, on the yoke seam of the shirt on page 54, the cording is basted to the bodice.
The cording should lie inward so the raw edges of cording and fabric are together and the stitching on the cording lies on the seamline of the garment.

6 Baste the two pieces of the garment together with the cording enclosed between the layers. Sew on the seamline so that the stitches follow the line of stitching on the cording made in step 4. Press the seam allowances up and finish the raw edges.

Paul Williams

Binding center front and sleeve openings

Center front and sleeve openings can be bound for a neat and easy finish. They are usually cut to a curved "keyhole" shape so that the binding, which is cut on the bias, can be shaped around the curved edge and lies smoothly when finished.

Center front and sleeve openings should be bound before the side or sleeve seams of a garment are sewn so that you can work with the fabric flat.

The finished width of the binding can vary but is usually $\frac{1}{4}$-$\frac{1}{2}$in (6-12mm). The bias strip should be four times the finished width of the binding to allow the seam allowances to be the same width as the binding itself.

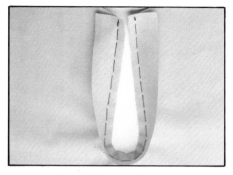

1 Cut a bias strip of fabric (see Volume 1, page 56) to fit around the opening.
Pin and baste the bias strip to the opening with right sides together and raw edges even, stretching the binding slightly around the curved edge of the opening. Sew the binding in place the same distance from the raw edge as the finished width of the binding.

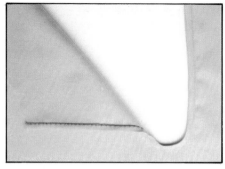

2 Press the binding over the seam allowance, taking care not to stretch the binding. Fold in a seam allowance on the free raw edge of the binding equal to the finished width of the binding. Slip stitch the binding to the line of stitching. Press.

Softly suited

This silk shirt, with corded yoke seams and a separate scarf, teams up with the skirt in Volume 7, page 79.

Adapting the pattern

Measurements

The shirt is made by adapting the pattern for the shirt from the Pattern Pack, available in sizes 10-20, which correspond to sizes 8-18 in ready-made clothes.

Materials

2 sheets of tracing paper 36 x 24in (91 x 61cm); flexible curve

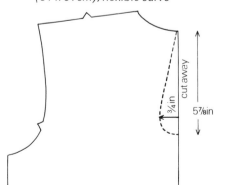

1 Trace the shirt front, front and back yoke and sleeve pattern pieces. Mark a point on the center front line $5\frac{7}{8}$in (15cm) down from the neck edge. Use a flexible curve to shape the bottom of the neck opening. The curve should not be more than $\frac{3}{4}$in (2cm) at the widest part.

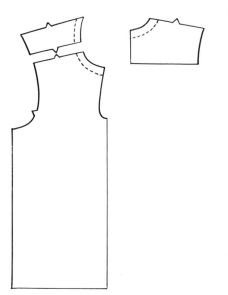

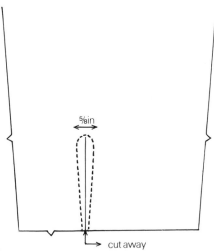

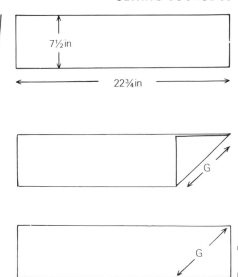

Terry Evans

2 Trim away the seam allowance at the neck edge on the shirt front, front yoke and back yoke pieces. The neck edge will be bound.

3 Reshape the top of the sleeve opening into a slight keyhole in the same way as the neck, making it approximately ⅝in (1.5cm) wide at the widest point as shown above.

4 Draw a rectangle 22¾ × 7½in (57.5 × 19cm) wide for the scarf. Fold one short end up to meet the long edge to find the true bias. Mark this diagonal line as the straight grain line.

Directions for making

Suggested fabrics
Challis, crepe de chine, wool crepe, lawn.

Materials
*36in (90cm)-wide fabric with/
without nap:
Sizes 10, 12 and 14: 3½yd (3.1m)
Sizes 16, 18 and 20: 3⅝yd (3.3m)
45in (115cm)-wide fabric with/
without nap:
Sizes 10, 12 and 14: 3⅛yd (2.8m)*

*Sizes 16, 18 and 20: 3¼yd (2.9m)
4in (10cm) lightweight interfacing
Three ½in (1.3cm) buttons; thread
⅝yd (.5m) yarn or narrow cord*

Key to adjusted pattern pieces
1	Shirt front	Cut 1 on fold
2	Shirt back	Cut 1 on fold
3	Front yoke	Cut 4
4	Back yoke	Cut 2
8	Sleeve	Cut 2
9	Cuff	Cut 2
A	Scarf	Cut 2

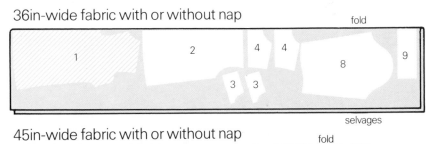

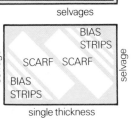

36in-wide fabric with or without nap

fold

1   2   4 4   8   9

3 3

selvages

45in-wide fabric with or without nap

fold

1   2   8

3 3   9   4

selvages

Layout for scarf and bias strips
for both widths of fabric

selvage

BIAS STRIPS

SCARF SCARF

BIAS STRIPS

selvage

single thickness

Tony Boase

John Hutchinson

55

Tony Boase

1 Alter the pattern pieces for the shirt front, front and back yokes and sleeve and draw the pattern for the scarf as shown on pages 54-55.

2 Prepare fabric and pin on pattern pieces as shown in layout for width of fabric being used. If you are using silk, follow directions in Volume 7, page 76 for pinning on and cutting out pieces. Open out the remaining fabric and pin on and cut out scarf piece twice, as shown in layout. Cut out two bias strips 8in (20cm) long and $1\frac{5}{8}$in (4cm) wide for front yoke seam cording and one piece $9 \times 1\frac{5}{8}$in (23×4cm) wide for cording back yoke seam. Cut two bias strips 9×1in (23×2.5cm) for binding neck, one piece $12\frac{5}{8} \times 1$in (32×2.5cm) for binding center front opening, and two pieces $8\frac{5}{8} \times 1$in (22×2.5cm) for binding the cuff openings.

3 Transfer all markings from the pattern pieces to the fabric.

4 Fold, baste and sew the bust darts with right sides together. Press them down.

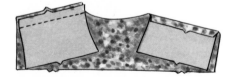

5 Baste and sew the front and back yoke pieces together at the shoulder seams with right sides together. Finish the seams and press open.
Sew the yoke facing pieces together the same way.

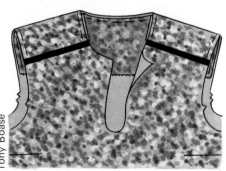

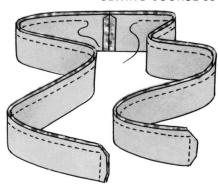

6 Baste the bias strips for the cording around the cord. Baste the cording to the shirt front and back on the yoke seamlines (see page 53). Baste and sew the yoke and bodice pieces together with right sides facing so the cording is caught securely in the seam. Face the yokes (see Volume 3, page 55) to enclose the seam and cording seam allowances.

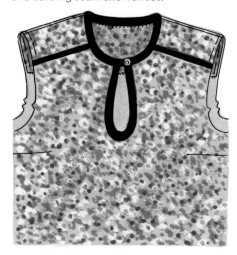

7 Bind the center front opening as shown on page 54. Join the two bias strips for the neck edge and bind this edge the same way as the center front opening. Sew a small button to the left side of the binding and make a thread loop on the right side (see Volume 7, page 66).

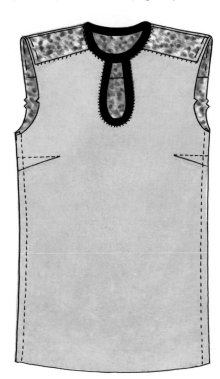

8 Baste and sew the side seams using French seams with tissue paper if you are working on silk fabric (see Volume 7, page 76). Press the seams to the back.

9 Bind the sleeve openings as shown on page 54. Baste and sew the underarm seams of the sleeves using French seams. Fold the pleats into place on the lower sleeve edge and baste. Interface half of each cuff and sew the interfaced edge of each cuff to the sleeves with right sides together. Fold the cuffs in half, right sides together, and sew across the short ends. Trim seam allowances and clip corners. Turn cuffs right side out, fold in raw edges and slip stitch in place.

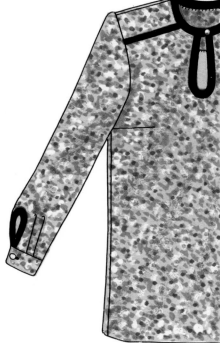

10 Run two rows of gathering stitches between the notches on the sleeve cap. Pin the sleeve into the armhole with right sides together and pull up the gathers so that the fullness is evenly distributed. Baste and sew the seam. Trim the seam allowance to $\frac{1}{4}$in (6mm) and finish the raw edges with small machine zig-zag stitches or hand overcasting. Repeat for other sleeve.

11 Turn up the hem edge of the shirt using the narrow hem method shown in Volume 1, page 65.

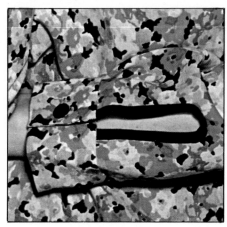

12 Join the two scarf pieces at the center back, with right sides together. Press seam open. Fold scarf in half lengthwise, right sides together. Sew across one short end and to within 1$\frac{3}{4}$in (4.5cm) of the center back seam on the long edge. Sew the other side of the scarf the same way. Trim the seam allowances, clip the corners and turn the scarf right side out. Baste around scarf close to the edge. Turn in the seam allowances of the opening and slip stitch to close. Press and remove basting.

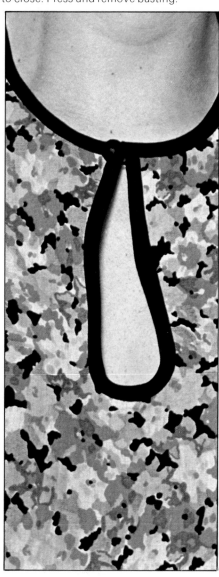

Shoestring

Quilted director's chair

Sit back and relax in this bright-colored director's chair.

Materials
- ¾yd (.7m) of 48in (120cm)-wide upholstery fabric
- Matching sewing thread
- ¾yd (.7m) of 48in (120cm)-wide thin foam
- Tailor's chalk
- Long ruler
- Pins
- 20 upholstery tacks
- Hammer

1 Press fabric well.
2 Cut one piece of fabric to measure 48×14¼in (120×36.5cm) and another to measure 48×8¼in (120×21cm). Cut foam to the same measurements.
3 To make the seat, fold large piece of fabric in half with right sides together to measure 24×14¼in (60×36.5cm).
4 Fold large piece of foam to measure 24×14¼in (61×36.5cm). Place foam on wrong side of fabric. Pin and baste in place through all four layers.
5 Stitch ½in (1.2cm) in along two long sides and one short side. Trim and grade seams as necessary.
6 Turn right side out so that the foam is "sandwiched" between the two layers of fabric.
7 To finish raw edge, cut away surplus foam, turn under raw edge and slip stitch together.
8 Mark evenly-spaced quilting lines with lines of basting at 4½in (12.5cm) intervals in both directions.
9 Stitch quilting lines, starting and stopping 1in (2.5cm) from the edges. Stitch long sides first and then short sides.
10 To make the back, fold small piece of fabric in half with right sides together to measure 24×8¼in (60×21cm). Fold small piece of foam in half to measure 24×8¼in (60×21cm).
11 Repeat steps 4-7 to make back.
12 To quilt the back, mark evenly spaced quilting lines with lines of basting at 4½in (12.5cm) intervals from one long edge to the other. Stitch four rows of quilting.
13 Turn under short edges 1¾in (4.5cm) at each end and slip stitch securely in place to make a channel for anchoring the

Ron Kelly

fabric back to the chair back.
14 Tack through fabric back and wooden uprights on the back of the chair, spacing upholstery tacks at 2in (5cm) intervals.

15 To attach the chair seat to the frame, tack upholstery tacks along the bottom edge of the seat support, spaced about 2in (5cm) apart.

*Button fly front
*Pants cuffs
*Tapered pants:
  adapting the pattern;
  directions for making

Button fly front

A button fly front makes an attractive alternative to a zipped placket. It is, however, not as strong as a zipper, so it is not really suitable for pants that need to be very hard-wearing.

Remember that fly fronts on women's pants should lap right over left and on men's pants, left over right. These directions are for women's pants.

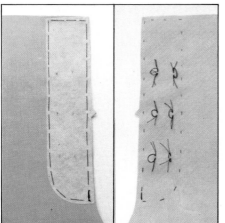

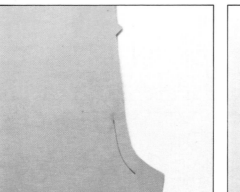

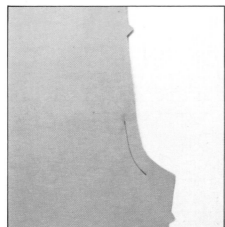

1 Transfer the position of the buttonholes to the right pants front using tailor's tacks.
Cut one piece of interfacing for the fly facing and baste it to the wrong side of the right center front opening of the pants, matching the notches together.

2 Stitch the front crotch seam from the circle to within 1⅜in (3.5cm) of the inside leg seam. Clip the curve and press the seam open.

3 Finish the curved edge of the fly facing with machine zig-zag stitches or overcasting.

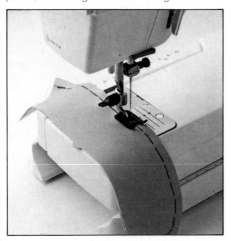

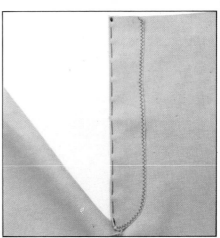

4 Baste and stitch the two remaining fly facing pieces together around the curved edge, taking ¼in (6mm) seam allowances and making sure right sides are together. This forms the fly shield.

5 Grade the seam allowances, clip into the curve and turn the shield right side out. Baste close to the stitched edges and press flat.

6 Baste and stitch the single fly facing to the right center front from the circle to the waistline. The notches should match and right sides should be together. Press the seam allowance toward the facing. Turn the facing to the inside and baste close to the stitched edge. Press.

continued

Paul Williams

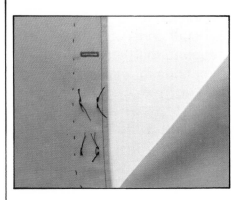

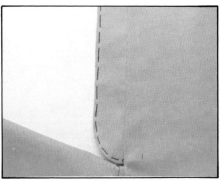

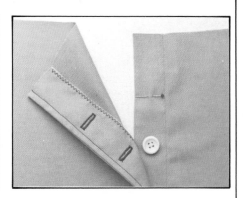

7 Topstitch the facing ¼in (6mm) from center front edge, working from the right side of the fabric.
Make three buttonholes by hand or machine in the positions marked by the basting.

8 Baste the fly shield to the left front with right sides together and the notches matching. Stitch in place from the circle to the waistline. Press only the seam allowance toward the pants so that the fly shield extends from the front edge. Understitch the pants to the seam allowance, close to seamline. Press.

9 Lap the right pants front over the left, matching the center fronts together. Mark the positions for the buttons beneath the buttonholes. Sew the buttons to the fly shield in the positions marked.

Pants cuffs

Cuffs on pants are formed by making a deep hem, part of which is folded to show on the right side as a design detail.

On straight legged pants the side and inside leg seams are stitched in a virtually straight line, but on tapered pants, like the ones on pages 61 and 63, the cuff is

wider at the top fold than at the hem fold to follow the taper of the pants, and the seam must zig-zag to follow this shape when finished.

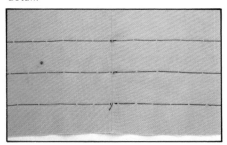

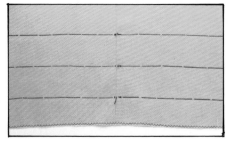

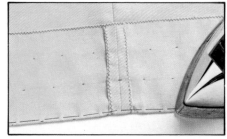

1 Transfer all fold lines from the pattern to the fabric with lines of basting stitches. These lines should match together when the side and inside leg seams are sewn.

2 Finish the lower edge of both pants legs with overcasting or zig-zag machine stitches if you are using fairly thick fabric, or by turning under ¼in (6mm) and stitching close to the fold if you are using lightweight fabric.

3 Fold the pants leg on the top foldline of each leg with the right sides of the fabric together. Baste close to the folded edge and press.

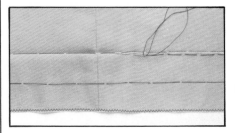

4 Fold the fabric down on the second fold-line so that the wrong sides of the fabric are together. This is the top fold of the cuff. Baste close to the folded edge and press.

5 Turn up the hem allowance to the inside of the pants leg on the last foldline and baste close to the lower hem edge through all the thicknesses of fabric. Sew the hem allowance to the pants on the inside with invisible hemming stitch. Press the lower hem edge only.

6 Fold the top edge of the cuff to the right side and catch-stitch the inside of the cuff only to the pants leg.

Paul Williams

All set for spring

Made in a lightweight fabric, these tapered pants will be an ideal addition to your spring wardrobe.

Measurements

These tapered pants are made by adapting the pattern for the pants from the Stitch by Stitch Pattern Pack, available in sizes 10-20, which correspond to sizes 8-18 in ready-made clothes.

Adapting the pattern

Materials

Two sheets of tracing paper at least 48 x 20in (122 x 50cm)
Flexible curve; yardstick

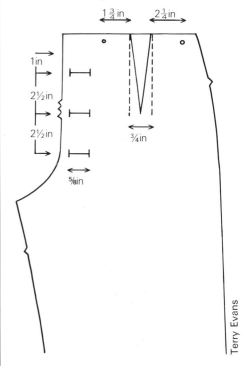

1 Trace the pants front. On the traced pattern, measure out $\frac{3}{8}$in (1cm) on both sides at the base of the dart and mark these points. Join the points to the dart lines at the waist edge to form the two lines for the tuck. Mark the tuck as a folding toward the center front with an arrow on the pattern.

2 For the positions of the pocket flap mark two points: the first $1\frac{3}{4}$in (4.5cm) toward center front from inner tuck line and the second $2\frac{1}{4}$in (5.5cm) toward side seam from outer tuck. Mark both points on the seamline.

3 Mark three buttonholes from the center front seamline, the first 1in (2.5cm) from the waist seamline and the other two at $2\frac{1}{2}$in (6.5cm) intervals from the first. Mark the buttonholes $\frac{5}{8}$in (1.5cm) long for $\frac{1}{2}$in (1.3cm)-diameter buttons. You may need to adjust this length depending on the buttons available.

Gary Warren

Terry Evans

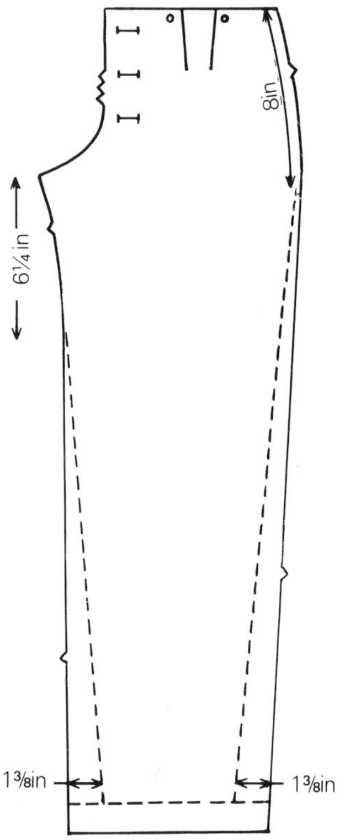

4 Trace the back pants piece. On both the front and back pattern pieces, measure in 1$\frac{3}{8}$in (3.5cm) from cutting lines at the hemline and mark these points. Mark hipline 8in (20.5cm) below waist on the side edge and join this point to the point at the hemline. Measure down 6$\frac{1}{4}$in (16cm) from crotch point and join this point to the point at the hem line on the inside leg. The two lines just drawn are the new side and inside leg cutting lines.

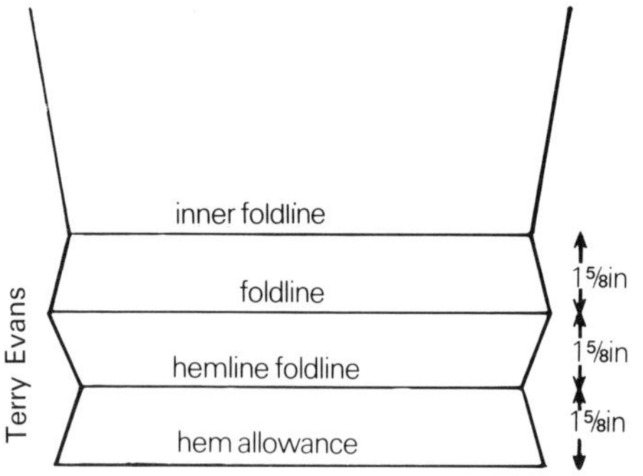

Terry Evans

5 On both pattern pieces draw in the cuffs as follows: measure down 1$\frac{5}{8}$in (4cm) from the pants hemline—which becomes the first foldline—and draw a line to mark the fold at the top of the cuff. Measure down another 1$\frac{5}{8}$in (4cm) and draw another line to mark the foldline for the hem. Measure down a further 1$\frac{5}{8}$in (4cm) and mark this line as the cutting line. To shape the side seams of the cuffs fold them in place on the lines marked. Using a ruler, continue the inside and outside seams downward to the folded hemline. Cut along these lines and unfold the cuffs to see the shaping.

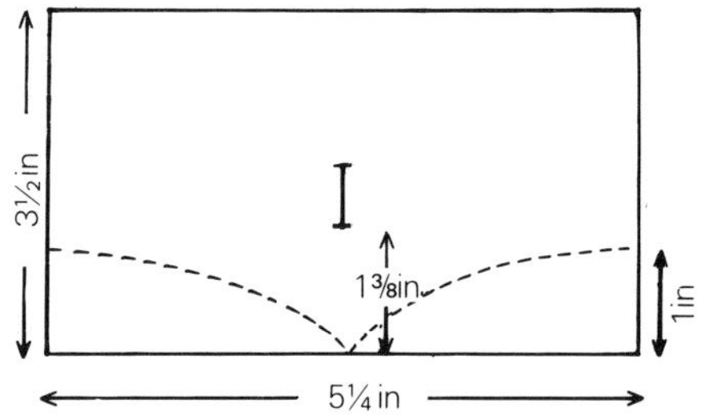

6 Draw a rectangle 5$\frac{1}{4}$in (13cm) wide and 3$\frac{1}{2}$in (9cm) deep as basis for pocket flap. Draw a line vertically to mark center of rectangle. At side edges of rectangle measure up 1in (2.5cm) and mark these points. Draw a curve from one side edge to the base of the center line, either free hand or using a flexible curve. Fold the rectangle in half down the marked line and trace the curve. Cut along these lines for the finished shape of the pocket flap. $\frac{5}{8}$in (1.5cm) seam allowances have been included on all sides. Mark a $\frac{5}{8}$in (1.5cm) long buttonhole on center line, 1$\frac{3}{8}$in (3.5cm) from point.

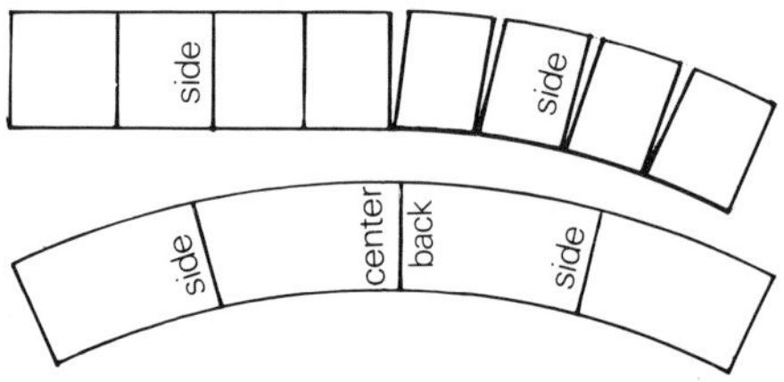

7 Trace the waistband pattern, making it $\frac{5}{8}$in (1.5cm) narrower than original pattern piece. Mark the center front and center back lines by tracing them from the original waistband. Mark the notches for the side seams in the same way. Draw a line midway between each set of points so that the waistband is divided into 8 sections.
Slash along these lines from the top edge of the waistband to the seamline at the waist edge. Measure around your body 2$\frac{1}{2}$in (6.5cm) above your natural waistline. Compare this measurement to the measurement of the original waistband. The difference is the amount that the waistband must be let out, so open each slash an equal amount until the top seamline on the waistband measures the same as your body measurement. Tape paper under the slashes.

8 It is advisable to cut the waistband out in muslin to check the fit and make any adjustments if necessary. If the waistband is too big, pin out the fullness equally at each slash. If the waistband is too small, snip into each slash and insert muslin under the slashes until the waistband fits. Draw the new waistband pattern piece from the muslin one. Mark the center back and side positions on the paper pattern. The center back pattern piece should be marked to be placed on the straight grain.

Directions for making

Suggested fabrics
Wool worsted, corduroy, wool or synthetic gabardine.

Materials
36in- (90cm-) wide fabric with or without nap:
Size 10: 3yd (2.7m)
Size 12: 3$\frac{1}{8}$yd (2.8m)
Size 14: 3$\frac{1}{4}$yd (2.9m)
Size 16: 3$\frac{3}{4}$yd (3.4m)
Size 18: 3$\frac{7}{8}$yd (3.5m)
Size 20: 4yd (3.6m)
45in- (115cm-) wide fabric with or without nap:
Sizes 10 to 16: 3$\frac{1}{8}$yd (2.8m)
Sizes 18 and 20: 3$\frac{1}{4}$yd (2.9m)
54in (140cm)-wide fabric without nap:
Size 10: 1$\frac{3}{4}$yd (1.6m)
Size 12: 1$\frac{7}{8}$yd (1.7m)
Size 14: 2yd (1.8m)
Size 16: 2$\frac{1}{8}$yd (1.9m)
Size 18: 2$\frac{1}{4}$yd (2m)
Size 20: 2$\frac{3}{8}$yd (2.1m)
36in- (90cm-) wide interfacing:
Sizes 10 to 18: $\frac{3}{8}$yd (.3m)
Size 20: 1$\frac{1}{8}$yd (1.1m)
Six $\frac{1}{2}$in (1.3cm) buttons; thread

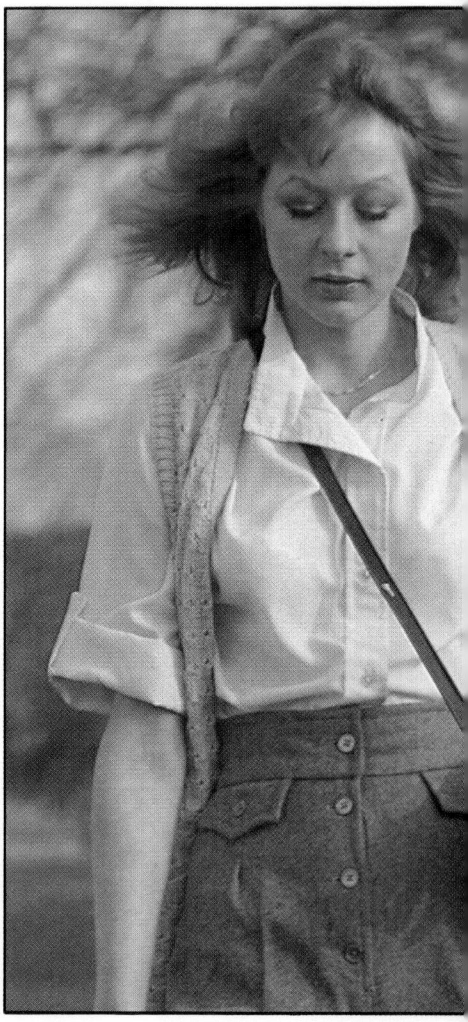

Gary Warren

1 Alter the pattern pieces for the pants and draw the pocket flap pieces as shown on pages 61-62.

2 Make any necessary alterations to the new pattern pieces. For difficult fitting problems (see Volume 2, page 64) it is advisable to make a shell from muslin and make any adjustments to this. Transfer any alterations to the pattern pieces. Check that the pants length is correct as this pattern includes cuffs which are difficult to adjust once the pattern has been cut out.

3 Prepare the fabric and pin on the pattern pieces, following the appropriate layout for the fabric you are using. Make sure that the straight grain line on the pattern is on the correct grain on the fabric. Cut out the pieces carefully.

4 Transfer all markings from the pattern pieces to the fabric.

5 Cut out the waistband, fly facing and pocket flap pieces from the interfacing as shown in the layout for your size.

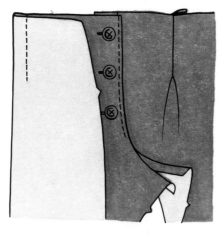 

Terry Evans

6 Make the button fly front as shown on pages 59-60.

7 Fold the two tuck lines together on each pants front and baste and stitch from the bottom of the tuck to the waist edge. Secure the thread ends and press the tucks outward.

8 Topstitch $\frac{1}{4}$in (6mm) outside the tuck line and across the bottom of the tuck, stitching through all thicknesses of fabric. Secure the thread ends. Press.

Cutting layout

36in-wide fabric with or without nap

fold

2

POCKET FLAPS 4 4 cut 1

3

selvages

45in-wide fabric with or without nap

fold

2 1

4 4

cut 1
POCKET FLAPS

3

selvages

Key to adjusted pattern pieces

1	Pants front	Cut 2
2	Pants back	Cut 2
3	Waistband	Cut 2
4	Fly facing	Cut 3
A	Pocket flap	Cut 4

Interfacing
Pieces 3 and 4—cut 1
Piece A—cut 2

54in-wide fabric without nap

fold

2 POCKET FLAPS 3

4
4
cut 1

1

selvages

36in-wide interfacing for sizes 10 to 18

fold

3
4 ←cut 1

selvages

for size 20

fold

4 ← cut 1

3

selvages

John Hutchinson

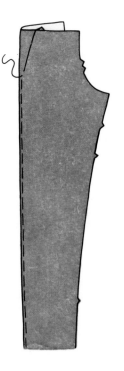

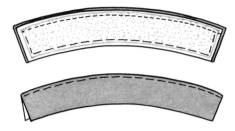

16 Baste the interfacing to the wrong side of one waistband piece. Baste and stitch the two waistband pieces together with right sides facing. Grade the seam, trimming the interfacing close to the stitching. Turn the waistband right side out and baste close to the seam. Press.

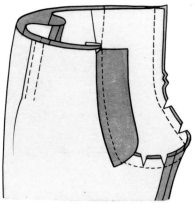

13 Turn one leg inside out and slip it inside the other so that the right sides are together. Match the notches and the inside leg seams and baste and stitch the crotch seam from the fly facing to the back waist edge. Clip the curves and press the seam open.

9 Fold, baste and sew the waist darts on each pants back. Press the darts toward the center. Mark the crease lines on the pants pieces as shown in Volume 2, page 63.

17 Baste and sew the waistband to the pants with right sides together, securing the flaps in the seam. Press the seam toward the waistband. Baste and stitch the short edges of the waistband with right sides together. Grade the seam and cut across the corners.

18 Turn under the seam allowance on the inside waistband and baste and slip stitch in place. Press. Topstitch $\frac{1}{4}$in (6mm) in from the outer and center front edges of the waistband. Sew buttons to pants beneath flaps. Mark button and buttonhole position and make buttonhole in waistband.

14 Baste interfacing to the wrong side of two pocket flap pieces. Baste and stitch an interfaced pocket flap to an uninterfaced pocket flap leaving the long straight edge open. Grade the seam, trimming the interfacing close to the stitching and cut across the corners. Turn the flap right side out and baste close to the stitched edges. Press flat. Topstitch $\frac{1}{4}$in (6mm) from outer edges of the flap. Make a buttonhole by hand or machine in the position marked. Repeat for the second pocket flap.

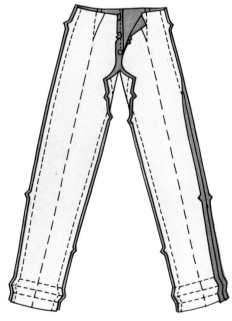

10 Baste the side, inside leg and back crotch seams of the pants with the right sides of fabric facing. Try on the pants and check the fit. Make any adjustments and check that the crease lines hang straight (see Volume 2, page 64).
11 Remove the basting from the back crotch seam and the inside leg seams and stitch the side seams.
Finish the seams and press them open.
12 Re-baste and sew the inside leg seams, easing in the fullness between the back notches to fit those on the fronts. Finish the seams and press open.

15 Baste the flaps to the pants fronts at the positions marked with the raw edges level.

19 Turn up the pants hems into cuffs as described on page 60.

Sewing / COURSE 35

* Working with even stripes cut on the bias
* Fabric belt carriers
* Bias cut skirt: adapting the pattern; directions for making

Working with even stripes cut on the bias

If the pieces of a garment are cut on the bias they have more "give" and will drape well. If an evenly striped fabric is cut on the bias, an attractive chevron pattern is formed where the seams of the garment are joined. This breaks the plainness of the vertical stripes and highlights the seaming of the garment, as shown in the skirt featured on page 71.

Collars, cuffs, bindings and pockets cut on the bias can all become features on a garment when the remainder of the garment is cut on the straight grain.

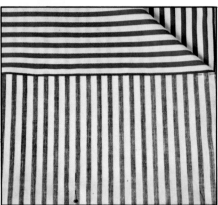

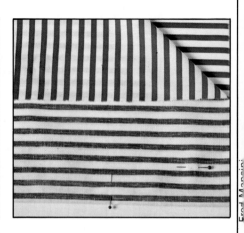

1 To cut out a garment on the bias, fold the fabric in half either lengthwise or crosswise, depending on the cutting layout for your pattern.

If the fabric is folded lengthwise, fold and pin exactly down the center of one stripe, if the stripes are vertically printed or woven. Make sure that the stripes on the top layer are exactly over the same stripes lying underneath. Pin the matched stripes together at intervals along the fold, across the two raw edges and down the selvage.

2 If the fabric is folded crosswise it is prepared in the same way, pinning at intervals across the fold, down the two selvages and across the raw edge.

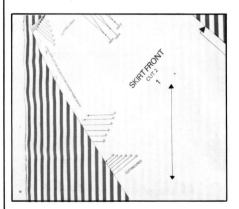

3 Place pattern pieces for bias-cut garments with grain lines on the straight grain as usual, parallel to the selvage, which means that the pattern piece itself will be lying at an angle to the selvage.

4 Make sure that the notches which will be matched together are lying on the same stripe. The stripes should be matched on the seamline, not the cutting line, at the waistline, armholes, sleeves, side, center and shoulder seams.

5 The seams of the garment should be slip-basted (see Volume 6, page 69) so that the stripes can be matched exactly. This will also help to prevent them from moving while they are being sewn. Stitch from the hemline upward to prevent the fabric from stretching and distorting—this is always important if the fabric is cut on the bias but is advisable with any shaped skirt.

Fabric belt carriers

Simple tube belt carrier

These simple tubular belt carriers are easy to make and can be used on any garment where you need secure belt carriers. They are usually about ⅜in (1cm) wide, but this can be varied and will depend on the fabric you are using—the heavier the fabric the wider the carrier will need to be. The length of the carrier will depend on the width of the belt to be used.

They may be used at the side seams of the waist of dresses, but if the belt is to be made of the same fabric as the dress it is more usual to use the less obtrusive thread belt carriers described in Sewing course 30, Volume 7, page 66.

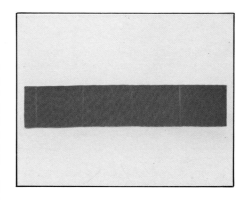

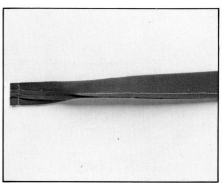

1 To make the fabric tube, cut a strip of fabric twice the width required plus ½in (1.2cm) for seams. Measure the belt or waistband that the carrier is to cover, allowing slight ease, and add ¾in (2cm) for seams to this measurement. Cut a strip of fabric long enough to make the number of carriers required to the total length calculated.

2 Fold the strip in half lengthwise with right sides together and stitch ¼in (6mm) in from raw edge. Trim seam allowance to ⅛in (3mm). Ease seam to center of strip and press seam allowances open with your fingers. Sew across one short end of strip ¼in (6mm) from end.

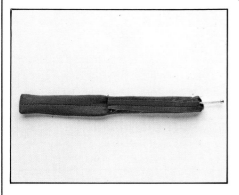

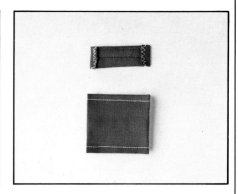

3 Turn stitched end of strip to inside of tube and, with a ball-point needle, gently push tube right side out.

4 Cut off the stitched end and ease the seam once more to the center of the strip. Press flat. Cut the strip into the lengths needed for each carrier.

5 Turn in ¼in (6mm) at ends and finish raw ends with overcasting. If the carriers are very wide, they can be topstitched before attaching them to the garment.

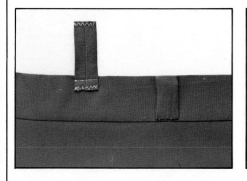

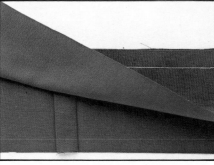

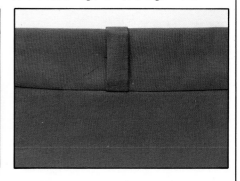

6 To attach a carrier to a finished waistband, position the carrier on the band at the position marked. The carrier end should overlap top edge of waistband by ⅜in (1cm). Sew across carrier ¼in (6mm) from raw edge making sure stitches do not continue onto waistband. Backstitch to hold carrier down and fold under ⅜in (1cm). Either slip stitch carrier in place or topstitch it in position close to the fold.

7 To attach carriers to a waistband in the seam, baste them in position at the waistband, flat against the band as shown above. Lay the second waistband piece over the first to cover the carriers. Baste and sew the top and end seams in the usual way.

8 Baste the carriers in position at the raw edge of the waistband, allowing some slackness so that the belt will fit through the finished carrier easily. Baste and stitch the waistband to the skirt with right sides together, securing the carriers in the seam. Finish the waistband in the usual way. With this method, the waistband is not topstitched.

Shaped belt carriers

These shaped belt carriers, like the simpler tubular belt carriers, may be used to hold a belt in place at the waistline, of a dress, coat, skirt, pants or shorts. The simple shape forms a decorative feature in the design of the garment. Commercial paper patterns usually give pattern pieces for the carriers, but if you wish to add carriers to a garment you can draw your own pattern piece as we have in step 5 on page 70.

The size of the carriers will depend to a certain extent on the type of fabric you are using—a lightweight cotton dress will not take very large carriers—about 1in (2.5cm) wide is probably ample—while a heavy coat, made from fairly bulky fabric, will have to have larger carriers—about 2in (5cm) wide should be suitable.

The shape will depend on the design of the garment and the position of the carriers. In the step-by-step photographs we have used carriers for a waistband, shaped at one end and sewn into the waistband. If the carriers had been on a coat or jacket, it would have been possible to shape them at both ends and topstitch them in place, rather than sewing them into the waistband.

The number of carriers will again depend on the design of the garment. In the skirt shown here, it was only necessary to use four carriers. In some cases, particularly on coats or jackets, it may be necessary to use six carriers. It is usually advisable to position the carriers at a seamline, so that they do not interrupt the lines of the garment, but this may not always be possible.

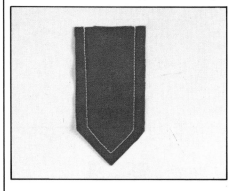

1 Baste and sew two shaped carrier pieces together leaving one end open for turning. This is usually the end that is sewn into the waistband seam. Trim seam allowances and clip into them where necessary.

2 Turn right side out and baste close to stitched edges. Press flat and topstitch $\frac{1}{4}$in (6mm) from the edges.

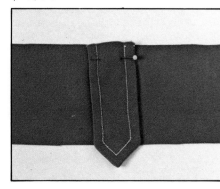

3 Pin the carriers to the waistband in the positions indicated on the pattern with the raw edges of the carriers along the edge of the waistband.

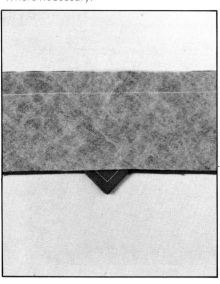

4 Lay the second waistband piece and interfacing over the first and baste and sew the top seam in the usual way, catching the carriers in the seam. Trim the interfacing close to the stitching and grade the seam allowances. Turn the waistband right side out and baste along the stitched edge. Press the carriers downward.

5 Baste and sew the waistband to the skirt with right sides together, keeping the ends of the carriers free of the seam. Turn the waistband to the wrong side, turn under the raw edge of the waistband facing and slip stitch in place. The waistband can be topstitched if desired.

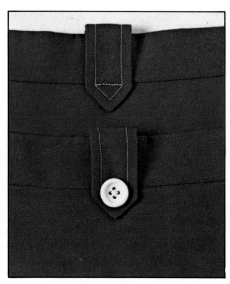

6 The carriers can be topstitched in place or, as on the skirt on page 69, the carriers can be fastened with buttons.

Smart skirts for city slickers

These A-line skirts are made from eight panels for an evenly flared effect. The panels are cut on the bias to give a crisp tailored look.

If the skirt is made in an even-striped fabric, it is possible to create an attractive chevron effect, with the stripes matching and balancing at each seam. Pointed belt carriers emphasize the seamlines at front and back.

Adapting the pattern

Measurements
The skirt is made by adapting the pattern for the A-line skirt from the Stitch by Stitch Pattern Pack, available in sizes 10-20, which correspond to sizes 8-18 in ready-made clothes.

Materials
Sheets of tracing paper at least 33 x 25in (85 x 65cm)
Transparent tape
Right triangle
Ruler or yardstick

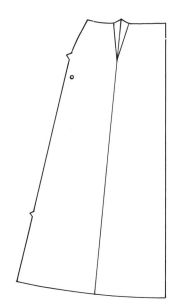

1 Lay a sheet of tracing paper over the skirt front pattern. Trace the skirt front. Draw a line through the center of the waist dart and continue the line downward to the hemline. This line indicates where to open up the pattern in step 2.

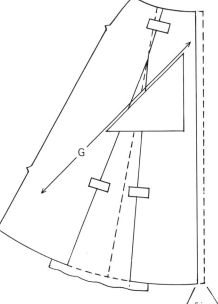

2 Cut along the marked line as far as the dart point.

Close the dart top by matching the dart lines together and tape in place. This will open up the skirt, so tape tracing paper behind the slash.

Draw a line $\frac{5}{8}$in (1.5cm) outside the center front line to give you the seam allowance. The next step is to mark the grain line. Place the triangle at right angles to the center front, so that one short edge lies parallel to the center front line. Draw along the sloping side of the triangle to mark the grain line on the pattern, extending it so that both sections of the pattern are marked.

If you want to mark a bias grain line on a pattern piece without a straight edge to it, position the triangle so that one short edge is on the existing grain line and mark the new grain line down the sloping edge in the way described in the previous paragraph.

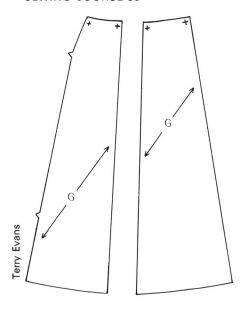

Terry Evans

3 Mark a point halfway across the waistline and another point halfway

across the hemline. Join the two points. Cut along this line to divide skirt front into two pieces—front panel and side front—as indicated in diagram. Add $\frac{5}{8}$in (1.5cm) seam allowances to new edges.

4 Trace the skirt back and divide the pattern into the side back and back panel in exactly the same way as for the skirt front, marking the new grain lines.

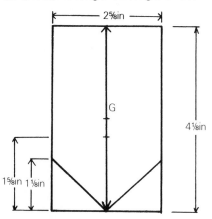

5 Draw a rectangle $4\frac{1}{8}$in (10.5cm) tall and $2\frac{5}{8}$in (6.5cm) wide to make belt carrier pattern. Mark center vertically on rectangle for grain line. Measure up $1\frac{1}{8}$in (3cm) from bottom line on both sides of rectangle and join these points to grain line where it meets bottom edge. Seam allowances of $\frac{5}{8}$in (1.5cm) have been included in these measurements. Cut out pattern piece and mark a $\frac{1}{2}$in- (1.3cm-) long buttonhole on grain line $1\frac{5}{8}$in (4cm) from the point where the grain line meets the bottom edge, as shown.

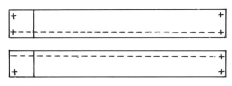

6 Trace the waistband pattern piece to the horizontal foldline only and add $\frac{5}{8}$in (1.5cm) seam allowances to the long edge above the foldline. Cut out the pattern piece.

Directions for making

Suggested fabrics
Single knits, lightweight wool tweed, flannel, wool challis.

Materials
36in- (90cm-) wide fabric with or without nap:
   Sizes 10 and 12: 3$\frac{3}{4}$yd (3.4m)
   Size 14: 4yd (3.6m)
   Size 16: 4$\frac{3}{8}$yd (4m)
   Sizes 18 and 20: 4$\frac{5}{8}$yd (4.2m)
45in- (115cm-) wide fabric with or without nap:
   Size 10: 3$\frac{1}{4}$yd (2.9m)
   Size 12: 3$\frac{1}{3}$yd (3m)
   Sizes 14 and 16: 3$\frac{1}{2}$yd (3.1m)
   Size 18: 3$\frac{5}{8}$yd (3.3m)
   Size 20: 3$\frac{3}{4}$yd (3.4m)
36in- (90cm-) wide interfacing:
   Sizes 10-16: $\frac{1}{4}$yd (.2m)
   Sizes 18 and 20: $\frac{3}{8}$yd (.3m)
7in (18cm) skirt zipper
Hook and eye; thread
Four $\frac{3}{8}$in (1cm) buttons

Key to adjusted pattern pieces
1 Skirt front panel		Cut 2
2 Skirt side front		Cut 2
3 Skirt back panel		Cut 2
4 Skirt side back		Cut 2
Waistband		Cut 2
Belt carriers		Cut 8

Interfacing
Use waistband pattern piece

1 Alter the skirt pattern and draw the pattern for the belt carriers as shown on page 69 and above.
2 Prepare the fabric and pin on the pieces, making sure you follow the correct layout for your fabric width.

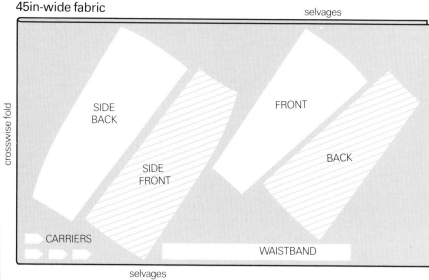

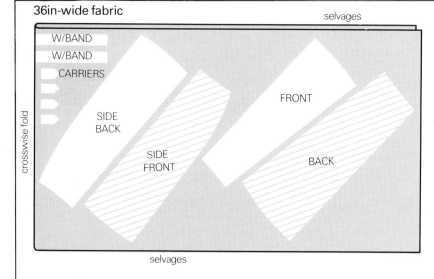

Brian Mayor

3 Transfer all markings from the pattern to the fabric using tailor's tacks or tailor's chalk.
4 Cut out the waistband piece once from interfacing.

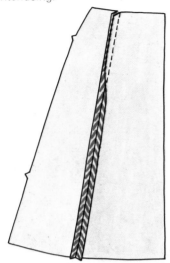

5 Baste and stitch one side front to a front panel, with right sides together. Repeat with the other two pieces for the skirt front. Stitch the two front panel pieces together. Assemble the skirt back the same way.

6 Baste and stitch the skirt front to the skirt back with right sides together, leaving the left seam open above the dot for inserting the zipper. Press the seams open and finish allowances with overcasting or machine zig-zag stitch.

7 Baste and stitch the zipper into the opening using the lapped seam method as shown in Volume 2, page 45.

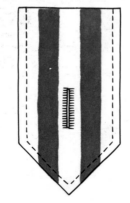

8 Baste and stitch the belt carrier pieces together in pairs. Clip corners, and trim seam allowances. Turn right side out and topstitch as shown on page 68. Sew a buttonhole on each carrier in the position marked.

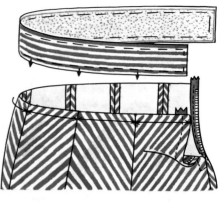

9 Pin and baste the interfacing to the wrong side of one waistband piece. The belt carriers are positioned above the four panel seams in the skirt. Measure from the left side seam of the skirt to the first front panel seam. Measure this distance from end of waistband and mark with a pin, subtracting the $\frac{5}{8}$in (1.5cm) seam allowance before measuring. Measure between the first and second panel seams and mark this measurement on the waistband in the same way. Measure around to the back panel seams and transfer these measurements to the waistband so that you can match the marks to the seamlines.

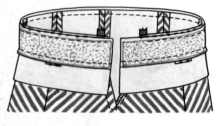

10 Baste the carriers to the waistband and sew the two waistband pieces together as described on page 68. Baste and stitch the waistband to the skirt with right sides together, keeping the carriers free of the seam. Stitch across the short ends of the waistband and turn band right side out.

11 Fold under the raw edge and slip stitch in place. Attach skirt hook and eye to waistband above zipper opening. Sew a button to the skirt under the buttonhole on each belt carrier.
12 Try on the skirt and mark the hem. Turn up the hem and finish the raw edge. Sew the hem in place using invisible hemming stitch and taking in any fullness by making tucks if necessary. Press the folded edge of the hem only.

Victor Yuan

Terry Evans

*Italian quilting
*Quilted housecoat:
  adapting the pattern;
  directions for making

Italian quilting

Italian quilting is purely decorative and does not provide warmth in a garment. It consists of parallel lines of stitches sewn by hand or machine, through which cord, thick knitting yarn or specially manufactured quilting yarn is threaded. This raises the fabric and throws the pattern into relief.

Soft, pliable fabrics are best suited to this type of quilting. Satin is very effective when quilted in this way, for the sheen helps to emphasize the lines of the design. The quilting is backed with soft cotton such as chambray or gauze so that the cord or yarn can be threaded into the channels from the wrong side of the work, using a tapestry needle. The quilted sections of the garment are lined to conceal the underside of the work. Sometimes—as in the housecoat overleaf—the quilted sections are worked separately and then applied to the garment.

1 Transfer the stitching lines for the quilting from the pattern to the right side of the fabric using tailor's chalk, dressmaker's carbon paper or lines of basting.

2 Place the backing fabric on the wrong side of the fabric and baste the two layers together, making a grid of basting stitches over the whole area to be quilted to prevent the fabrics from slipping.

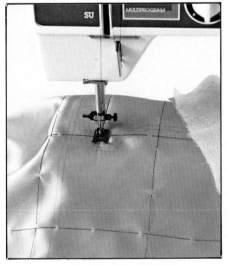

3 Sew along the marked lines with either small hand-sewn back stitches or straight machine stitching. Remove the basting.

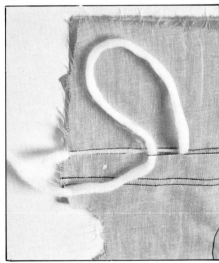

4 Thread a tapestry needle with the yarn or cord being used, making sure that the yarn is slightly longer than the channel through which it will be threaded. With the backing fabric facing up, insert the needle through the backing fabric at the beginning of one channel and push it through the channel without piercing the top fabric.

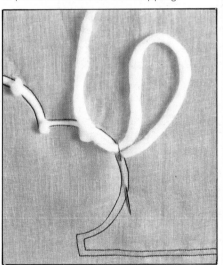

5 At sharp angles and on curves, bring the needle out of the backing fabric and re-insert it, leaving a small, uncut loop. This will prevent the fabric from puckering and will allow for shrinkage if the garment is washed.

Paul Williams

73

Lady of leisure

An elegant housecoat for those precious moments when you're alone . . . or with someone special.

Adapting the pattern

Measurements

The housecoat is made by adapting the pattern for the jacket from the Stitch by Stitch Pattern Pack, available in sizes 10-20, corresponding to sizes 8-18 in ready-made clothes.

Materials

3 sheets of tracing paper 24 x 67in (60 x 170cm)
Yardstick
Flexible curve

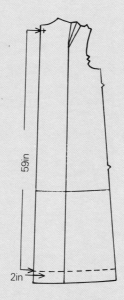

1 Decide on the finished length for the housecoat. The yardage given is for a garment 59in (150cm) long, so if you wish to make the housecoat longer than this, allow extra fabric.
Trace the jacket back pattern leaving enough paper to extend the side seams downward. Extend the center back line and side seamline to the required length. Mark new hemline by measuring down from original hemline across pattern. Add 2in (5cm) hem allowance to lower edge of back.

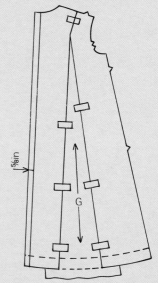

2 Add a $\frac{5}{8}$in (1.5cm) seam allowance to center back edge. Draw a line parallel to center back from shoulder dart point to the lower edge of the pattern. Slash up the dart line to the dart point. Close the

dart and tape in place to open out the lower edge of the pattern. Insert paper under the slash and tape it in place. Draw in the hemline between the two edges of the pattern and draw in the straight grain line through the center of the slash.

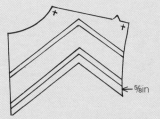

5/8in

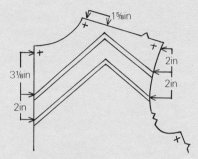

1 5/8in

3 1/8in

2in

2in

2in

3 Measure 3 1/8in (8cm) down center back from neck seamline and mark this point. Mark a second point 2in (5cm) lower down center back.
Mark a point 1 5/8in (4cm) out from neck seamline on the shoulder seamline. Mark a second point 2in (5cm) below the first. On the armhole, mark a point 2in (5cm) from shoulder seamline. Mark a second point 2in (5cm) lower down.
For the top line of stitching, connect the top three points from the center back to the shoulder and the shoulder to the armhole. This forms a chevron. Connect the points for the lower line of stitching in the same way. Draw in a line 1/4in (6mm) below each of the lines just drawn to mark the quilting channels.

4 Trace the top section of the back pattern to the last line for the quilting. Add 5/8in (1.5cm) seam allowances to lower edge and mark center back (excluding seam allowance) to be placed on the fold.

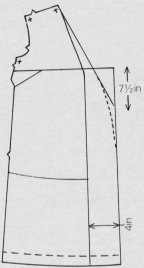

7 1/2 in

4in

5 Trace the front jacket pattern and extend the pattern downward in the same way as for the back.
Draw a line 4in (10cm) from and parallel

to front cutting edge to form new front line. Extend the hemline. Extend the top line of the bust dart to meet the new front line. Mark a point 7 1/2in (19cm) down from bustline on front line. Join this point to the shoulder seamline on the neck edge. Draw a soft curve where the two lines meet, using a flexible curve.

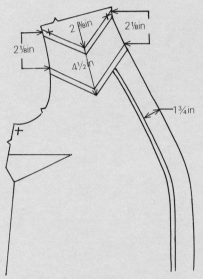

2 1/8in

2 3/8in

2 1/8in

2 1/8in

4 1/2in

1 3/4in

Terry Evans

6 To mark the stitching lines for the quilting, draw a guideline perpendicular to the center of the shoulder line. For the top line, mark a point 2 3/8in (6cm) from shoulder seamline on the perpendicular guideline. Join this point to the corner where the shoulder and armhole seamlines meet. Then draw a line from the point to the corner where the shoulder and neck seamlines meet. For the bottom line of stitching mark a point on armhole and neck edges 2 1/8in (5.5cm) from shoulder seamline. Mark a point 4 1/2in (11.5cm) from shoulder seamline on the perpendicular guideline. Connect these three points in the same way as for the first stitching line. Draw in a second stitching line 1/4in (6mm) below each of the lines for quilting channels.

Jay Myrdal

75

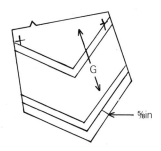

7 Trace the shoulder area of the front to the lowest stitching line. Add ⅝in (1.5cm) seam allowance to lower edge and draw straight grain line parallel to the front edge. This is the front yoke.

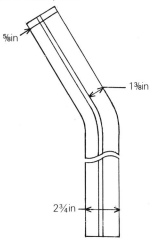

8 Trace the front edge curve of the housecoat from the last quilting line at the shoulder to the hem edge. Draw a line 2¾in (7cm) in from edge to form front facing. Draw first quilting line 1⅜in (3.5cm) from outer edge down whole length of the facing. Draw second quilting line ¼in (6mm) from first, toward the inner edge. Add a ⅝in (1.5cm) seam allowance to the top edge and draw the straight grain line parallel to the front edge.

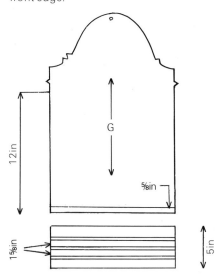

9 Extend lower edge of sleeve pattern by 12in (30cm) and connect these lines

for the new sleeve lower edge. Mark the new seamline ⅝in (1.5cm) up from the lower edge.

Draw a rectangle 5in (12.5cm) deep by the width of the sleeve at the lower edge for the sleeve facing.

For the quilting stitching lines, draw parallel lines at intervals of ¾, 2⅜ and 4in (2, 6 and 10cm) from lower edge. Draw in second channel lines ¼in (6mm) above each of these lines.

10 Draw a rectangle 31¼ × 2¾in (79.5 × 7cm) for tie belt pattern piece.

Directions for making

Suggested fabrics

Satin or satin back crepe, wool or synthetic crepes, Viyella®, lightweight wool, brushed cottons, with a matching or contrasting fabric for the yoke, sleeve, front facing and tie belt pieces.

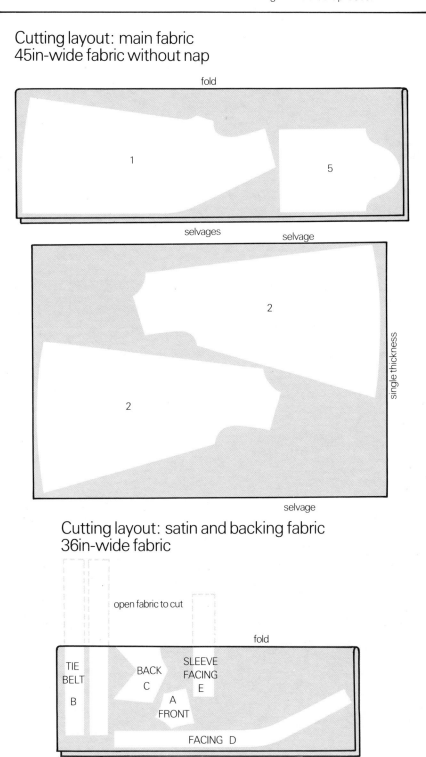

Cutting layout: main fabric
45in-wide fabric without nap

Cutting layout: satin and backing fabric
36in-wide fabric

John Hutchinson

Materials

45in- (115cm-) wide fabric without nap:
Sizes 10, 12, 14: 4¾yd (4.30m)
Sizes 16, 18, 20: 5½yd (5m)
36in- (90cm-) wide satin or contrast fabric without nap:
For all sizes: 1⅞yd (1.7m)
36in- (90cm-) wide backing fabric:
For all sizes: 1⅞yd (1.7m)
Matching thread
8yd (7.5m) of quilting yarn, 8 ply knitting yarn or thin cord
1⅛yd (1m) matching bias binding

Key to adjusted pattern pieces

1	Housecoat front	Cut 2
2	Housecoat back	Cut 2
5	Sleeve	Cut 2
A	Front yoke	Cut 2 each in satin and backing fabric
B	Tie belt	Cut 2 in satin
C	Back yoke	Cut 1 on fold in satin Cut 1 on fold in backing fabric
D	Front facing	Cut 2 each in satin and backing fabric
E	Sleeve facing	Cut 2 each in satin and backing fabric

1 Alter the pattern pieces for the housecoat and draw the new pattern pieces as shown on pages 74, 76.
2 Prepare the main fabric and pin on the pattern pieces for the front, back and sleeve as shown in the layout given. Make sure that the straight grain line on the pattern lies on the straight grain of the fabric. Cut out the pieces.
3 Pin on and cut out the back yoke, front yoke, sleeve and front facing and tie belt from satin as shown in the layout.
4 Pin on and cut out the first four pieces from step 3 in backing fabric.
5 Transfer the markings from the pattern pieces to the fabric. Transfer the lines for the quilting with tailor's chalk, dressmaker's carbon paper or basting.

6 Fold, baste and stitch the bust darts. Press downward.

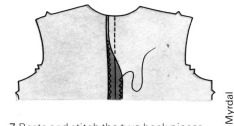

7 Baste and stitch the two back pieces together at the center back seam with

right sides together. Press the seam open and finish the raw edges.
8 Baste the backing fabric pieces to the wrong side of the yoke front, yoke back, sleeve and front facings (see page 73).

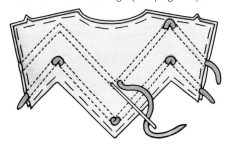

9 Sew the lines for the quilting by hand or machine and thread the yarn or cord through the channels as shown on page 73.

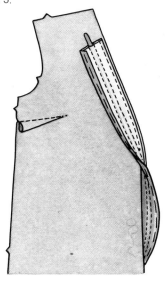

10 With right side of front facing on wrong side of housecoat, working up from the

lower edge, baste and stitch the outer edge of one satin facing to the corresponding front section of the housecoat. Grade the seam allowances and press the facing towards the housecoat. Turn under the seam allowance on the inner edge of the facing; baste and slip stitch in place. Repeat for the remaining satin facing.
Press carefully to avoid flattening the quilting.

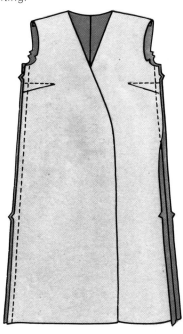

Terry Evans

11 Baste and stitch the front and back housecoat pieces together at the shoulder and side seams with the wrong sides of the fabric together at the shoulder seams and the right sides together at the side seams. Finish the seams with overcasting or zig-zag machine stitching and press open, avoiding flattening quilting.

Jay Myrdal

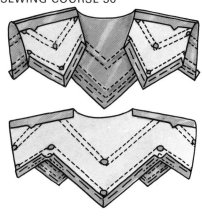

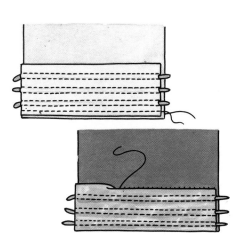

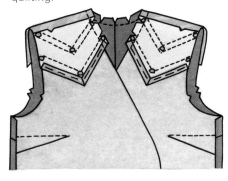

12 Baste and stitch the back and front yoke pieces together at the shoulder seams with right sides together. Stay-stitch the back yoke at the two inner points of the shape. Turn under ⅝in (1.5cm) seam allowance on lower edges of the yoke pieces, clipping almost to the stay-stitching on the back yoke. Baste and press flat, taking care not to flatten quilting.

13 Baste and stitch the yoke to the housecoat around neck edge with the right side of the yoke next to the wrong side of the housecoat and the neck edges even.
Trim the seam allowance and clip the curves. Press the seam allowance toward the housecoat.

14 Turn the yoke to the right side and baste close to the stitched neck edge. Press. Baste the yoke to the housecoat around the armholes and lower edges. Slip stitch in place close to the folds at the lower edges, taking small stitches and keeping the hem even. Press.

15 Baste and stitch the sleeve facings to the sleeves with the right sides of the facings to the wrong sides of the sleeves, and raw edges even. Press the seam open and then carefully press the facing to the right side.
Turn in ⅝in (1.5cm) seam allowance on upper edge of sleeve facing. Slip stitch in place close to the fold.

16 Sew two rows of gathering stitches around the sleeve cap between the notches. Baste and stitch the underarm seam of the sleeve, making sure the quilting lines are matched. Press the seam open and finish the raw edges.

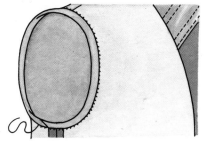

17 Pin and baste the sleeve into the armhole, pulling up the gathering threads so that the fullness is evenly distributed. Sew the seam with the sleeve on top. Press the seam allowance toward the sleeve and clip the curves. Trim seam allowances to ¼in (6mm) and finish edges with bias binding.

18 Join the two belt pieces together along one short edge. Press the seam open. Fold the belt in half lengthwise with right sides together and baste and stitch ⅝in (1.5cm) from the ends and long raw edge, leaving a 6in (15cm) opening at center of long edge. Trim the seam, clip across the corners and turn belt right side out. Fold in the seam allowance and slip stitch across the opening. Baste around the edges and press. Make thread belt carriers (see Volume 7, page 66) at waistline at side seams.

19 Try on the housecoat with the belt tied and mark the hem. Turn up and baste the hem close to the fold. Turn under ¼in (6mm) on raw edge and machine stitch close to fold. Sew the hem in place using invisible hemming stitch. Fold the facing back to the inside and slip stitch to the hem allowance. Press the folded edge of the hem only.

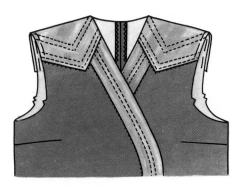

Terry Evans

Jay Myrdal

Sewing / COURSE 37

Lined patch pockets

Lining patch pockets helps give more body when a lightweight fabric is being used. It also improves the appearance of pockets if they are made in an opaque fabric or if the outside pocket piece has been decorated, as the lining hides the wrong side of the work.

The lining can be cut from the same fabric as the pocket itself, unless a very bulky fabric is used; lightweight lining fabric or cotton are suitable alternatives.

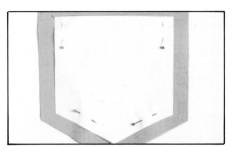

1 Cut out pocket and lining using same pattern piece. If you make your own pattern, add $\frac{5}{8}$in (1.5cm) seam allowances all around finished shape of pocket. Trim away $\frac{1}{8}$in (3mm) around lining piece.

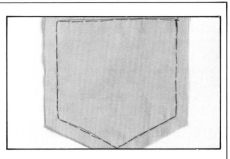

2 Baste the lining and pocket together with right sides together and raw edges even, so that lining is still smaller than pocket. Stitch $\frac{5}{8}$in (1.5cm) from edges, leaving 2in (5cm) gap on one edge.

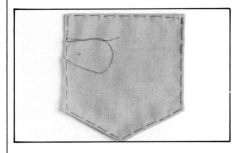

3 Trim the seam, clip the corners and turn the pocket right side out. Baste close to the seamed edges and slip stitch the opening.

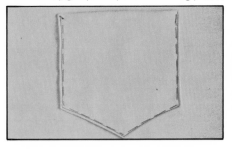

4 Pin and baste the pocket in place, after checking that it is correctly positioned by trying on the garment. Topstitch close to the side and lower edges to attach the pocket to the garment.

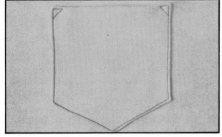

5 To reinforce the top corners of the pocket, form a small triangular shape at both top edges with topstitching. Start the stitching $\frac{3}{8}$in (1cm) below top pocket edge, sew diagonally toward the center of the pocket, back across the top edge and down the side edge of the pocket. Finish other corner in same way.

Lingerie strap guards

Lingerie strap guards are attached to the wrong side of a garment at the shoulder seams to catch the straps of underwear and prevent them from moving out of position and showing when sleeveless or low-cut garments are worn.

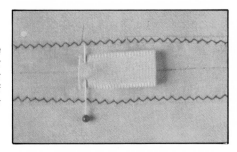

1 Cut two $1\frac{5}{8}$in (4cm) lengths of $\frac{1}{4}$in (6mm-) wide straight seam binding. Press $\frac{1}{4}$in (6mm) to wrong side at both ends of each tape. Center one tape along each shoulder seam as shown.

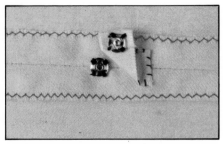

2 Hand-sew the end of the tape nearest the armhole to garment taking stitches through the seam allowances only. Sew the ball section of a snap to underside of free end of tape. Sew socket section of snap to shoulder seam allowances.

Elasticized waistbands

This type of waistband is usually used on skirts, shorts and pants which do not need a zipper or button fastening. An elasticized waistband makes clothes easy to put on and comfortable so is often used on children's wear and sportswear. Since the garment is pulled over the hips, the waist edge before elastic is attached must be larger than the hip measurement. The elastic is topstitched to the wrong side of the waistband after it has been joined to the garment. 1-2in (2.5-5cm) wide elastic is usually used.

The waistband may be cut in one or two pieces and joined either at the center back or at each side seam.

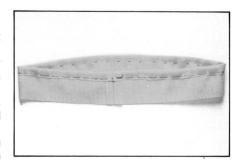

1 Join the waistband together at the short edges and press the seam or seams open. Fold under and baste down a $\frac{5}{8}$in (1.5cm) seam allowance at the top edge of the waistband. Press.

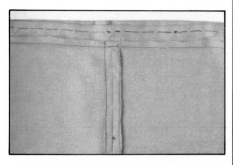

2 Baste and stitch the waistband to the garment with right sides together so that the center back, center front and side seams are aligned. Grade seam allowance and press the seam toward the waistband.

3 Cut a length of elastic to fit your waist comfortably, allowing an extra $\frac{3}{4}$in (2cm) for seam allowances. Join the short edges of the elastic.
Divide the elastic into four equal parts and mark with pins.

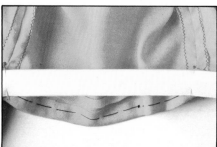

4 Pin the elastic to the waistband with wrong sides together and the pins matched to the center front, center back and side seam positions.
Stretch the elastic evenly between these pins and pin and baste elastic in place.

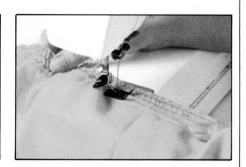

5 Start the stitching at the center back on each row, working on the right side. The first row should be close to the top edge and the next rows should be worked at $\frac{1}{4}$in (6mm) intervals from the first. Stretch the elastic as you machine stitch. Pull the thread ends through to the wrong side and finish off securely.

Satin stitch

Satin stitch is an embroidery stitch used for filling small areas of a design. The finished shapes have a sheen similar to satin because the stitches are sewn closely together. The stitches should not be more than about $\frac{1}{2}$in (1cm) long, as they will catch on jewelry and pull loose if they are longer.

The stitches may also be sewn by machine, if you have a zig-zag model. Use zig-zag stitch, adjusting machine to the widest stitch. Put the fabric to be embroidered in the embroidery hoop and insert it under the foot. (It may be necessary to take the foot off the machine in order to fit it in.) It is then possible to embroider the area, following the marked lines.

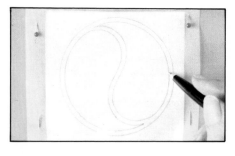

1a Transfer the design from the paper to the fabric using dressmaker's carbon paper. Lay the fabric with the right side facing up and pin the design paper in place. Insert the dressmaker's carbon paper, in a suitable color for the fabric, between the layers with the carbon side facing down. With a ballpoint pen, draw over the lines of the design. Remove the paper and the carbon.

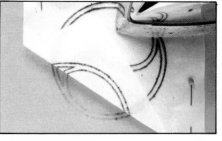

1b Or you can transfer the design with an embroidery transfer pencil. First draw the design on thin paper. Using the transfer pencil, trace the design on to the wrong side of the paper. This is most easily accomplished by taping the paper to a window. Sharpen the pencil if it becomes dull; thick lines will tend to "bleed" when the transfer is applied to the fabric. Pin the transfer in place and press over the design with a hot iron. Remove the paper and the design will be transferred to the fabric.

Fred Mancini

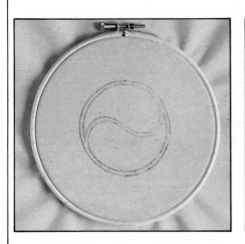

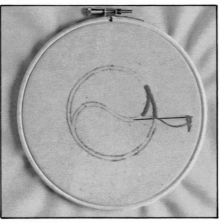

Fred Mancini

2 Insert the fabric into an embroidery hoop by laying it over the inner ring with the marked design facing up. Push the outer ring over the inner ring so that the fabric is secured between the two. Tighten the screw if the fabric is not held tautly.

3 Take the first stitch by bringing the needle out through the fabric on the marked edge of the design in the center of the shape. Take a straight stitch across the shape. Sew the next stitches in the same way, taking the needle down on the outer edge and bringing it up on the inner one. The wrong side of the work looks similar to the right side. You can also work the design in zig-zag stitch.

4 To finish, dampen the work and press lightly on the wrong side.

Tennis anyone?

This simple tennis outfit is just the thing. The top has a scoop neckline and buttons down the front, and the shorts have a sporty look, with contrasting binding on the legs, emphasized by the topstitching and contrasting buttons.

Measurements
The tennis outfit is made by adapting two patterns from the Stitch by Stitch Pattern Pack. The top is based on the T-shirt and the shorts are adapted from the pants pattern. The Pattern Pack is available in sizes 10 to 20, corresponding to sizes 8-18 in ready-made clothes. $\frac{5}{8}$in (1.5cm) seam allowances are included.

Adapting the pattern

Materials
Four sheets of tracing paper at least
20 x 31½in (50 x 80cm approx)
Cellophane tape
Flexible curve
Ruler or yardstick
Right triangle

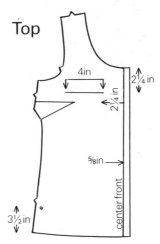

Top

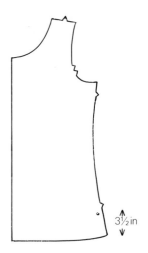

1 Trace the T-shirt front and add $\frac{5}{8}$in (1.5cm) seam allowance to the center front of the pattern.
Measure up 3½in (9cm) from the lower edge at the side seam and mark this as the top of the side slit.
Draw in a line at a right angle to the center front 2¼in (5.5cm) below neck cutting line and the same distance from the center front. Extend the line for 4in (10cm). This marks the position for the upper edge of the pocket, which is applied to the left side of the front.

2 Trace the T-shirt back and mark the side slit in the same way as for the front.

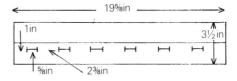

3 For front band, draw a rectangle 19⅝ × 3½in (50 × 9cm). Mark center front line 1⅛in (3cm) in from left edge and the

foldline $\frac{5}{8}$in (1.5cm) in from center front
line just marked. Measure down 1in
(2.5cm) from top edge on center front
line and mark top of first buttonhole.
Draw buttonhole $\frac{5}{8}$in (1.5cm) long and
mark five more buttonholes of the same
length at $2\frac{3}{8}$in (6cm) intervals down
center front. Draw in straight grain line
parallel to center front.

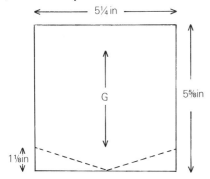

4 Draw a rectangle $5\frac{1}{4} \times 5\frac{5}{8}$in (13.5×14cm)
for the pocket. Measure up $1\frac{1}{8}$in (3cm)
from the bottom edge at both sides and
mark these points on the side edges. Join
to center point of base line.
5 Trace the front and armhole facing.
Mark the seam allowance $\frac{5}{8}$in (1.5cm) in
from the center front edge. The back neck
and armhole facing is not altered.

Shorts

1 Trace the top of the pants front
and back to the lower notches on the
inside leg seam, transferring all markings
to the new pattern piece.

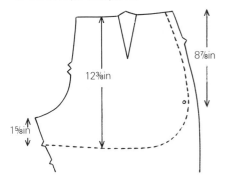

2 On the back, mark a point $1\frac{5}{8}$in (4cm)
down the inside leg seam from the crotch
seamline.
Extend the grain line to the waist edge
and mark a point $12\frac{3}{8}$in (31.5cm) down
from the waist seamline. Mark a point
$8\frac{7}{8}$in (22.5cm) from the waist seamline
on the side seam. This dot marks the base
of the side seam topstitching.
To establish the lower and side cutting
line, draw a line through the points on
the inside leg seam and grain line,
continuing the line to the side edge.
Reduce side seam allowance to $\frac{3}{8}$in (1cm)
and join side seam and horizontal line
with a flexible curve. Cut away excess.

82

Terry Evans

Victor Yuan

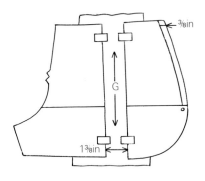

3 Cut along grain line and separate two pieces of pattern. Tape paper under slash so that two edges are 1⅜in (3.5cm) apart and line for lengthening and shortening is even on both sides. Draw a new grain line through center of slash. Omit waist dart.

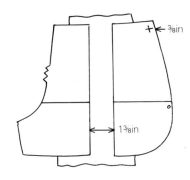

4 Make the same alterations to the front as to the back but make the measurement on the grain line only 12¼in (31cm). Waist dart is also omitted on shorts front.
5 Measure across the top edge of the front and back shorts pieces, between the seam lines. Add these measurements together, then add 1⅛in (3cm) for seams. Cut out waistband pattern piece to this measurement by 2¾in (7cm) wide.

Directions for making

Suggested fabrics
Lightweight gabardine, piqué, lightweight knits, satin (for shorts).

Materials
Top:
   36in- (90cm-) wide fabric with or
     without nap:
     For all sizes: 2¼yd (2m)
   45in- (115cm-) wide fabric without
     nap:
     For all sizes: 1⅝yd (1.4m)
   Matching sewing thread, topstitching
     thread, six ½in (1.3cm) buttons
Shorts:
   36in- (90cm-) or 45in- (115cm-) wide
     fabric with or without nap:
     For all sizes: 1⅛yd (1m)
   36in- (90cm-) wide fabric without
     nap for binding:
     For all sizes: ¾yd (.6m)

Matching sewing thread
Waist size plus seam allowance
   of 1½in- (3.5cm-) wide elastic
Top and shorts (from same fabric):
   36in- (90cm-) wide fabric with or
     without nap:
     Sizes 10 and 12: 3⅛yd (2.8m)
     Sizes 14 and 16: 3¼yd (2.9m)
     Sizes 18 and 20: 3⅓yd (3m)
   45in- (115cm-) wide fabric without
     nap:
     Sizes 10 and 12: 2¼yd (2.2m)
     Sizes 14 and 16: 2⅝yd (2.3m)
     Sizes 18 and 20: 2⅝yd (2.4m)
   36in- (90cm-) wide fabric without
     nap for binding:
     For all sizes: ¾yd (.6m)
   36in- (90cm-) wide interfacing
     For all sizes: ¾yd (.6m)
Matching sewing thread, topstitching

thread, six ½in (1.3cm) buttons
Waist size plus seam allowance of
   1½in (3.5cm-) wide elastic

Key to adjusted pattern pieces
Top:
1 Front		Cut 2
2 Back		Cut 1 on fold
3 Front neck and armhole facing		Cut 2
4 Back neck and armhole facing		Cut 1 on fold
A Front band		Cut 2
B Pocket		Cut 2

Shorts:
1 Front		Cut 2
2 Back		Cut 2
C Waistband		Cut 2

Interfacing
Use piece A to the foldline only

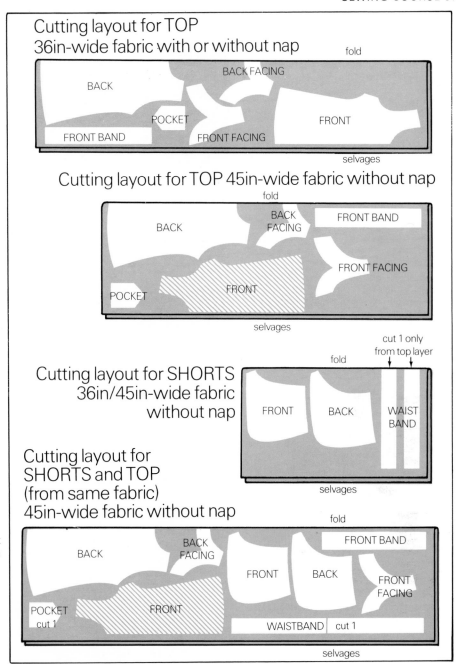

Cutting layout for TOP
36in-wide fabric with or without nap

fold

BACK
BACK FACING
POCKET
FRONT BAND
FRONT FACING
FRONT

selvages

Cutting layout for TOP 45in-wide fabric without nap

fold

BACK
BACK FACING
FRONT BAND
FRONT FACING
POCKET
FRONT

selvages

Cutting layout for SHORTS
36in/45in-wide fabric
without nap

cut 1 only from top layer

fold

FRONT
BACK
WAIST BAND

selvages

Cutting layout for SHORTS and TOP (from same fabric)
45in-wide fabric without nap

fold

BACK
BACK FACING
FRONT BAND
FRONT
BACK
FRONT FACING
POCKET
cut 1
FRONT
WAISTBAND
cut 1

selvages

John Hutchinson

1 Alter the patterns for the top and shorts and draw the new pattern pieces as shown on pages 81-83.

2 Prepare the fabrics and pin on the pattern pieces as shown in the appropriate layouts for your fabric widths. There is an alternative layout if you are making both the top and shorts from the same fabric.

If you are embroidering the pocket, cut out one pocket piece only using the pattern piece: this will be for the lining. For the pocket itself, cut out a 7in (18cm) square of fabric so that it will fit into an embroidery hoop. Cut it to pocket shape after it has been embroidered. Cut out the front band twice from interfacing, to the foldline only.

3 Cut out four bias strips 1⅝in (4cm) wide and 31½in (80cm) long from the fabric for the leg binding (see Volume 1, page 56).

4 Transfer all markings from the patterns to the fabric.

Top

1 Stay-stitch around the neck and armhole edges of the top front and back. Baste and stitch the bust darts and press them downward.

2 Baste the shoulder and side seams with the right sides of the fabric together and notches matching. Try on top and fit it carefully by pinning. Baste any altered side seams. Sew the side seams only, to the position marked for the top of the side slit. Press the seams open and finish the seam allowances.

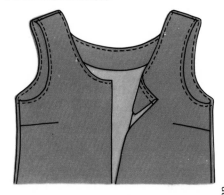

3 Rip out the shoulder seams and mark the new shoulder seamline if necessary with a line of basting on each side. Apply

Victor Yuan

the all-in-one facing to the neck and armhole edges as shown in Volume 4, page 63 leaving the centre front short edges unstitched. Do not understitch the facing to the seam allowance but baste close to the stitched edges. Press. Baste and sew the shoulder seams and join the seams of the facings as shown in Volume 4, page 64.
Topstitch around the neck and armhole edge ¼in (6mm) in from the edge. Press and remove basting.

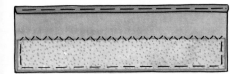

4 Baste the interfacing to the front band pieces and catch-stitch in place along foldline. Press flat.

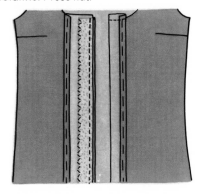

5 Baste and stitch the interfaced edge of one front band to the front edge with right sides together. Grade the seam, trimming the interfacing close to the stitching, and press the seam toward the band. Repeat with the second band.
Fold the bands on the foldlines with right sides together. Baste and stitch across the top of the bands, from the folded edge to the seamline. Trim the seams and cut across the corners. Turn bands right side out and baste close to folded edge.

6 Turn under ¼in (6mm) on lower edge of top, then a further ⅜in (1cm) to form a double hem. Baste and topstitch in place, starting at the seamline on the front band at each side. Press.
7 Fold under the raw edge of the front bands and slip stitch in place. Fold in raw edges at ends and slip stitch.

8 Sew the buttonholes by hand or machine on the right front band. Sew the buttons to the left front in corresponding positions.

Embroidered pocket

1 Transfer the motif for the embroidery to the center of the square fabric for the pocket using dressmaker's carbon paper. Insert the square into a small embroidery hoop and embroider the motif in satin stitch as shown on page 81. When the embroidery is complete, press the work on the wrong side. Cut out the pocket shape, centering the design under pattern piece.
2 Baste and stitch right sides of the two pocket pieces together as shown on page 79. Clip the corners, trim the seams and turn right side out.
Add two lines of topstitching across the top of the pocket.
Check that the pocket position is correct by pinning the pocket to the left side of the top and trying the top on. Make any adjustments and baste the pocket in place. Topstitch the pocket in place close to the side and lower edges. Secure the threads on the wrong side.

Shorts

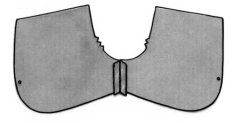

1 Baste and stitch right sides of one shorts back and front together at the inside leg seam. Finish the seam and press open. Baste and stitch the other back and front together in the same way.

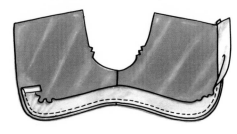

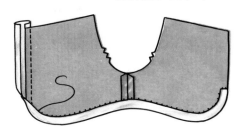

2 Join the bias strips to form two lengths of binding. Baste and stitch the bias binding to the outside edge of each leg piece with right sides together, taking the binding from the front waist edge to ¾in (2cm) above mark on back side seam. Press the binding to the wrong side, turn under ¼in (6mm) on short raw edge then turn under the long raw edge and slip stitch in place. Press.

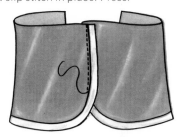

3 On one shorts piece lap the front over the back, matching the stitching line of the binding to the seamline on the back to form one leg. Baste and topstitch the seam from the mark on the back side seam to the waist, stitching just outside the seamline of the binding.

4 Baste and stitch the crotch seam with right sides together and the notches matching. Clip curved seam, finish seam allowances and press seam open.

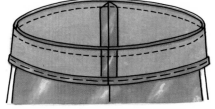

5 Join the waistband pieces at the side seams with right sides together. Press. seam open and finish seam allowances. Fold in the top edge of the waistband and baste down. Press. Baste and sew the waistband to the shorts, and attach the elastic as shown on page 80.

Terry Evans

Needlework / COURSE 11

*More needlepoint stitches
*Simple abstract designs
*Color and texture
*A container for dried flowers

More needlepoint stitches

Most of the needlepoint done today—as in the past—uses tent stitch. Being so small, it is especially useful for intricate curves and shading, such as in floral designs.

It's a pity, though, to confine your work to tent stitch when there are so many others to choose from—well over a hundred, in fact. These stitches give a textural interest that tent stitch lacks, and they can be combined in all sorts of ways to create fascinating effects. Many can be made larger or smaller by altering the number of threads worked over in each stitch; this allows for flexibility in filling in curves and other parts of a design. In this course we introduce three new stitches, which are used in the flower container on the opposite page. These are among the most often-used stitches, but you can find many others in books on needlepoint.

Flat stitch

Also known as cushion stitch, this is a very simple and effective stitch that can be varied in many ways. The blocks can be worked over different numbers of threads, they can be elongated by working over an extra horizontal thread and they can be combined with other stitches—as in Brighton stitch, far right. Here we show blocks worked in the same direction and in alternating directions. The alternating blocks make a more interesting pattern, but both stitches have a pleasing satiny texture that contrasts well with more nubbly stitches.

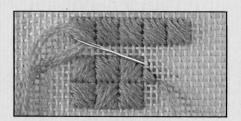

1 Here flat stitch is worked over four horizontal and four vertical threads (using three strands of crewel yarn on No. 12 canvas). The alternating blocks are worked in groups of four: top left, bottom left, top right (in progress), bottom right. Where possible—in any stitch—come up in an empty hole.

2 Brighton stitch This is basically a flat stitch with opposite corners cut off and combined with upright cross-stitches. Work the main stitch over two, three, four, three and two meshes successively. (In the sample the single mesh at the outer corners has also been covered, as in flat stitch, to fill the rectangular shape.) Add upright cross-stitches in the spaces.

Rice stitch

This versatile stitch is made up of two parts: a diagonal cross-stitch worked over an even number of threads (usually four) and smaller diagonal stitches worked over each arm of the cross. It can be worked in one color or in contrasting colors. Often the cross-stitch is worked in a fairly thick yarn and the small stitches in a fine one of a different type, such as pearl cotton or stranded embroidery floss. Contrasts of color and texture produce a lattice pattern, as in the second example at right.

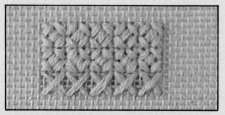

1 Here rice stitch is worked over four threads, using three strands of crewel on 12-mesh canvas. The cross-stitches should be worked, as usual, with the top stitches all slanting in the same direction, as can be seen in the bottom row. If using the same yarn and the same number of strands, as here, you can complete each stitch before beginning the next.

2 In this sample we have used four strands of crewel yarn for the cross-stitch and six strands of embroidery floss for the small stitches. In the stitch at top right, only the first small diagonal stitch has been worked; on the next row the second stitch has also been worked; and on the last row the third stitch has also been worked and the needle brought up, ready for the last stitch. This sequence may be varied, but the fourth stitch into a hole should always go *down* into it.

Frederick Mancini

Smyrna stitch

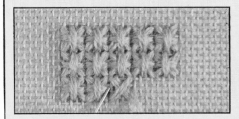 

1 This is another type of cross-stitch. A diagonal cross is worked over an even number of threads and then an upright cross is worked on top of it. Here Smyrna stitch has been worked over four threads using three strands of crewel yarn and 12-mesh canvas.

2 In this variation of Smyrna stitch the upright crosses on the larger stitches are worked over two threads instead of the four covered by the diagonal cross, and the horizontal stitch is uppermost. The spaces left between the stitches are filled with plain Smyrna stitch over two threads.

slide mount will serve the purpose. Move the finder slowly over the paper until it encloses a part of the design that works well on its own. Draw around this area. Trace the design and then enlarge it to the required size (see Volume 4, page 76), copying the shading from the original. You can also use this "finder" technique to find design possibilities in photographs.

What makes a good design is a complex question. There are certain basic rules, which apply to other visual arts as well as needlework, and anyone interested in doing original work should become familiar with them. But as in most arts and crafts, you can learn a lot about design simply by looking and doing.

Simple abstract designs

If you are one of the many embroiderers who work from kits because they doubt their ability to create an original design, the wealth of needlepoint stitches can open up exciting new possibilities for you. With textural variety even the simplest basic design becomes interesting. You needn't be able to draw in order to design any kind of embroidery (though drawing ability can be very useful); and this is particularly true in needlepoint, which is more concerned with shapes and textures than with line.

Look at the dried flower container shown here. Its design is extremely simple: a series of vertical and diagonal shapes given additional interest by the skillful use of color and texture. You can create a

similar design of your own; all you need is a sheet of paper of the correct proportions (see chart, overleaf), a ruler and a pencil. Draw a few perpendicular lines at irregular intervals, then add some diagonal lines to give a dynamic quality to the design.

Again using a ruler, you could try a slightly more complex design. Take a sheet of paper of any size and shape and draw lots of lines across it at various angles and intervals. Now cross these lines with others, again varying their direction and density. Now shade sections of the design, using pen or pencil, to get different tonal values. Don't worry about making a finished design at this stage.

Make a "finder"—a small cardboard frame with an opening the same shape as the finished embroidery. An empty color

Color and texture

The color scheme for the flower container has been kept very simple, partly to emphasize the variation in texture and partly so as not to conflict with the variety of colors in a mixed bouquet of flowers.

If you were using this design to cover a pencil holder or wastebasket you might use a more adventurous color scheme— for example, blue and green, or a neutral such as gray contrasted with bright red.

When you're first beginning to design, however, it's a good idea to keep your "palette" simple. You'll find that trying to balance shapes and tonal values offers enough of a challenge without tackling the complex relationships between different colors. A monochrome color scheme like this one can be enlivened by the use of a shiny thread, which gives yet more textural appeal.

Shades of gold

This versatile design, using three stitches, can be used to make an attractive container for dried flowers or to cover any other cylindrical object. We've made it in harmonizing shades of gold, but you might like to choose your own colors.

Victor Yuan

Size
The container measures 9¼in (23.5cm) in height and 3¾in (9.5cm) in diameter.

Materials
A piece of No. 14 mono canvas 13 x 18in (33 x 45cm)
*⅔oz (20g) each of three shades of crewel yarn (A, B and C)—the container shown uses Appletons' 475, 473 and 841; alternatively, use Persian yarn ***

1 skein of stranded embroidery floss to match shade B
No. 16 or 18 tapestry needle
A cylindrical cardboard tube, 9in (23cm) in height and 3¾in (9.5cm) in diameter; or a piece of strong but pliable cardboard 18in (46cm) square
A piece of cardboard 4 x 8in (10 x 20.5cm)
A ruler
A piece of felt, 9 x 17in (23 x 40cm), in a harmonizing color
A craft knife
A compass (optional)
Fabric glue
Masking tape
Sewing thread to match shade A and felt
A curved surgical needle, or ordinary sewing needle
Embroidery and sewing scissors
Materials for blocking (see Volume 1, page 75)
*(*Persian yarn, being thicker than crewel, will make the work thicker and slightly more difficult to mount.)*

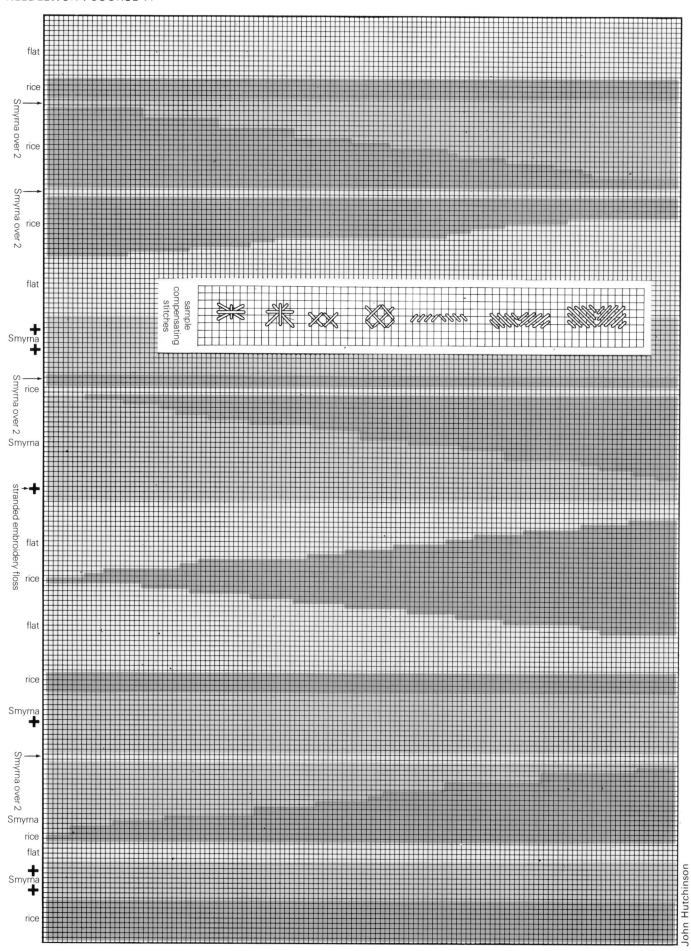

flat

rice

Smyrna over 2

rice

Smyrna over 2

rice

flat

Smyrna

rice

Smyrna over 2

Smyrna

stranded embroidery floss

flat

rice

flat

rice

Smyrna

Smyrna over 2

Smyrna

rice

flat

Smyrna

rice

sample
compensating
stitches

John Hutchinson

To work the embroidery

1 Bind the canvas edges with tape.
2 Measure up 2in (5cm) from the lower edge and the same distance from the left-hand side and begin working at this corner, using two strands of yarn and following the chart opposite. Note the symbols along the bottom of the chart showing where the top cross of Smyrna stitch is to be worked in stranded embroidery floss (six strands). For detailed instructions on working the stitches, see pages 86-87. Variations of the stitches used to fill narrow spaces—called compensating stitches—are shown on the chart. Continue along the bottom row to the last rice stitch at the lower right-hand corner.
3 Return to the lower left-hand corner and work alternating flat stitch up the left side until you have a total of 33 stitches.
4 Work the top row, following the chart, from left to right.
5 Now that you have set the pattern, begin filling it in, starting with the straight vertical sections and working upward from the bottom.
6 For the diagonal lines follow the chart, using compensating stitches as required, along the stepped diagonal lines. For the sake of simplicity the individual stitches are not marked; use your own judgement in selecting compensating stitches to fit the spaces.
7 When you have completed the embroidery, block it (see Volume 1, page 72).

To prepare the tube

Note If you are using a ready-made tube, follow steps 3, 4, 5, 7 and 8.
1 Bend the cardboard gently in both directions to find out which way it bends more easily. Using the craft knife, cut it in half in this direction. Trim one piece to measure 13½in (34.3cm) in length; the other (for lining) ⅛in (3mm) less.
2 Form each piece into a cylinder by butting the side edges together and joining them with masking tape. Slip the lining tube into the outer tube to make sure that it fits.
3 From the small piece of cardboard cut two circles, one 4in (10cm) in diameter for the bottom and the other, slightly smaller, for the lining bottom. (Use a compass or the lining tube as a guide in drawing the circles.)
4 Fix the larger circle to the bottom of the outer tube (or the ready-made tube) with masking tape.
5 Cover the inside of the lining tube (or the ready-made tube) with felt: cut a piece of felt 9 × 13in (23 × 33cm) and roll it up loosely. Spread a little glue over the inner surface of the tube (it need not cover the entire surface). Place the roll of felt in the tube and gently press it in place, carefully smoothing out any bumps and

Victor Yuan/designed by Mary Rhodes

wrinkles. Where one edge overlaps the other, fix it in place with a little more glue.
6 Slip the lining tube into the outer tube with the two joins well apart.
7 Cut two circles of felt, to fit the two cardboard circles.
8 Glue a felt circle to the smaller cardboard circle. Then apply glue to the uncovered side and press this into the bottom of the tube. There should not be any cardboard visible on the inside.

To mount the embroidery on the tube

1 Cut away all but ½in (1.2cm) along all four edges of the canvas. Cut out the four corners of this margin to eliminate bulk.
2 Fold under the unworked canvas along the top and bottom edges and also along the right-hand (rice-stitched) edge. Leave the left-hand edge flat.
3 Draw a vertical line in pencil on the tube. To ensure accuracy, use a plumb line (small weight on a string) as a guide.
4 Place the outer edge of the flat stitches along this line, with the canvas margin extending beyond it. Wrap the rest of the worked canvas around the tube, holding it firmly in position, but without using any glue. Carefully match the row of rice stitches to the row of flat stitches and sew

them together with sewing thread and (preferably) a curved surgical needle.
5 Make sure the vertical lines of the design are vertical on the tube, then sew the felt lining to the top of the work.
6 Glue the remaining felt circle to the bottom of the tube and sew its edges to the lower edge of the embroidery.

To adapt the design

By using smaller or larger gauge canvas you can alter the size of the container without changing the design. For example, No. 20 canvas will make the design about 6½in (16.5cm) tall (and correspondingly narrower), and No. 10 canvas will make it 13¼in (34cm) tall. To make the design much larger or smaller, use it simply as a guide and increase or reduce the number of stitches. Remember that you may also need to use a different thickness of yarn. Practice the stitches on your chosen canvas.

CROCHET

This V-neck sweater with fitted cuffs and elasticized hem is for the man who likes the casual look. It is worked in a distinctive two-colored cotton bouclé yarn.

Cool and casual

Victor Yuan

Sizes

To fit 36[38:40]in (92[97:102]cm) chest.
Length, 28[29:30]in (70[72:74]cm).
Sleeve seam, 17½[18:18½]in (45[46:47]cm), including cuff.
Note Directions for larger sizes are in brackets []; where there is only one set of figures it applies to all sizes.

Materials

23[25:27]x2oz (50g) balls of a medium-weight cotton bouclé
Sizes E and G (3.50 and 4.50mm) crochet hooks
½in (1cm)-wide elastic to fit around hips

Gauge

30 sts and 20 rows to 8in (20cm) over hdc on size G (4.50mm) hook.

Back

Using size G (4.50mm) hook make 81 [85:89]ch.
Base row 1hdc into 3rd ch from hook, 1hdc into each ch to end. Turn. 80[84:88]hdc.
Patt row 2ch to count as first hdc, skip first hdc, 1hdc into each hdc, ending with 1hdc into top of 2ch. Turn. Rep last row 68[70:72] times more. Fasten off.

Front

Work as given for back until 46 rows have been completed.
Divide for neck
Next row Patt across first 40[42:44] sts. Turn.
Next row 2ch, skip first hdc, leaving last loop of each on hook, work 1hdc into each of next 2hdc, yo and draw through all loops on hook—called dec 1, patt to end. Turn.
Next row Patt to end. Turn.
Rep last 2 rows until 28[29:30] sts rem. Fasten off.
Rejoin yarn to sts that were left as base of V, 2ch, patt to end. Turn.
Next row Patt to last 3 sts, dec 1, 1hdc into top of 2ch. Turn.
Next row Patt to end. Turn.
Rep last 2 rows until 28[29:30] sts rem. Fasten off.

Sleeves

Using size G (4.50mm) hook make 53[57:61]ch. Work base row as for back. 52[56:60] sts. Cont in patt as for back, inc one st at each end of every 5th row until there are 68[72:76] sts. Cont straight until sleeve measures 15[15½:16]in (39[40:41]cm). Fasten off.

Neckband

Join shoulder seams. With RS of work facing and using size E (3.50mm) hook, rejoin yarn to first row end on right front neck at base of V, work (1sc into next row end, 2sc into next row end) to shoulder, 1sc into each st across back neck, then (1sc into next row end, 2sc into next row end) down left front neck. Turn.
Next row 1ch, 1sc into each sc all around neck edge. Turn.
Rep last row 3 times more. Fasten off.

Cuffs

Using size E (3.50mm) hook work along foundation ch of sleeve by working (1sc into each of next 2ch, skip 1ch) to end. Turn.
Next row 1ch, 1sc into each sc to end. Turn.
Rep last row 10 times more. Fasten off.

To finish

Press lightly. Sew in sleeves. Join side and sleeve seams. Overlap right and left front neckbands at base of V and sew in place. Turn approx ½in (1cm) to WS at lower edge to form casing for elastic. Thread elastic through casing.

John Hutchinson

CROCHET

Summer nights, summer days

Something really special—a filet crochet jacket to wear over dresses on cool summer nights, or over swimsuits to set off your tan. Make it and wear it all summer.

Sizes
To fit 32-34[36-38]in (83-87[92-97]cm) bust.
Length, 24¾[25¼]in (63[64]cm).
Sleeve seam, 18in (46cm).
Note Directions for larger size are in brackets [ ]; if there is only one set of figures it applies to both sizes.

Materials
11[13] × 150yd (140m) balls of a lightweight mercerized crochet cotton
No. 7 (1.50mm) steel crochet hook

Gauge
9 sps and 8 rows to 3¼in (8cm) on No. 7 (1.50mm) hook.

Jean Claude Volpelière

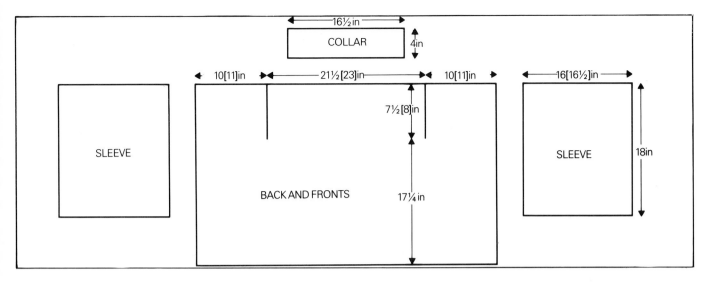

Main body

Using No. 7 (1.50mm) hook make 346[376]ch for entire lower edge.

Base row 1 tr into 5th ch from hook, 1 tr into each ch to end. Turn. 343[373] sts.

Next row 6ch, 1 tr into 4th tr, (2ch, skip next 2tr, 1 tr into next tr) to end, working last tr into top of the 4ch. Turn. 114[124] sps.

Next row 6ch, 1 tr into 2nd tr, (2ch, 1 tr into next tr) to end, working last tr into 3rd of the 6ch. Turn.

Reading RS rows from right to left and WS rows from left to right, following chart A for motifs, set patt as foll:

1st row 6ch, 1 tr into 2nd tr, (2ch, 1 tr into next tr) 13[15] times, *(2tr into next sp, 1 tr into next tr) twice – 2 blocks made –, (2ch, 1 tr into next tr) 26[28] times, rep from * twice more, (2tr into next sp, 1 tr into next tr) twice, (2ch, 1 tr into next tr) 14[16] times, working last tr into 3rd of the 6ch. Turn.

2nd row 6ch, 1 tr into 2nd tr, (2ch, 1 tr into next tr) 12[14] times, *2tr into next sp, 1 tr into each of next 7tr, (2ch, 1 tr into next tr) 25[27] times, rep from * twice more, 2tr into next sp, 1 tr into each of next 7tr, (2ch, 1 tr into next tr) 14[16] times, working last tr into 3rd of the 6ch. Turn.

3rd row 6ch, 1 tr, into 2nd tr, (2ch, 1 tr into next tr) 2[4] times, *(2tr into next sp, 1 tr into next tr) twice, (2ch, 1 tr into next tr) 8 times, 2tr into next sp, 1 tr into each of next 10tr, 2tr into next sp, 1 tr into next tr, (2ch, 1 tr into next tr) 13[15] times, rep from * to end omitting last 2ch and tr on last rep. Turn.

4th row 6ch, 1 tr into 2nd tr, (2ch, 1 tr into next tr) 11[13] times, *1 tr into each of next 7tr, 2ch skip next 2tr – 1 space made over 1 block –, 1 tr into each of next 7tr, (2ch, 1 tr into next tr) twice, (2tr into next sp, 1 tr into next tr) twice, (2ch, 1 tr into next tr) 4 times, 2ch, skip next 2tr, 1 tr into each of next 4tr, (2ch, 1 tr into next tr) 13[15]

times, rep from * to end, finishing last rep (2ch, 1 tr into next tr) 3[5] times. Turn.

Cont working from chart until 20th row has been completed. Work 4 rows in sps. Reading RS rows from right to left and WS rows from left to right, foll chart B for motifs, set patt as foll:

1st row 6ch, 1 tr into 2nd tr, (2ch, 1 tr into next tr) 13[15] times, *(2tr into next sp, 1 tr into next tr) 3 times, (2ch, 1 tr into next tr) 25[27] times, rep from * twice more, (2tr into next sp, 1 tr into next tr) 3 times, (2ch, 1 tr into next tr 13[15] times. Turn.

Cont working from chart until 16th row has been completed. Work 1 row in sps.

Divide for armholes

Next row (WS) 6ch, 1 tr into 2nd tr, (2ch, 1 tr into next tr) 28[31] times, turn. Work on these sts for left front. Work 2 rows in sps. Reading RS rows from right to left and WS rows from left to right, foll chart C for motifs, set patt as foll:

1st row 6ch, 1 tr into 2nd tr, (2ch, 1 tr into next tr) 11[12] times, (2tr into next sp, 1 tr into next tr) twice, (2ch, 1 tr into next tr) 15[17] times. Turn.

Cont working from chart until the 12th row has been completed. Now cont in sps only until work measures $24\frac{3}{4}[25\frac{1}{4}]$in (63[64]cm) from beg. Fasten off. With WS facing rejoin yarn to base of last tr before left front. Turn.

Next row 6ch, 1 tr into next tr, (2ch, 1 tr into next tr) 55[59] times. Turn. Work on these sts for back. Work 2 rows in sps. Reading RS rows from right to left and WS rows from left to right, foll chart C for motifs, set patt as foll:

1st row 6ch, 1 tr into 2nd tr, (2ch, 1 tr into next tr) 11[12] times, (2tr into next sp, 1 tr into next tr) twice, (2ch, 1 tr into next tr) 26[28] times, (2tr into next sp, 1 tr into next tr) twice, (2ch, 1 tr into next tr) 14[15] times. Turn.

Cont working from chart until the 12th row has been completed. Now cont in sps only until work measures $24\frac{3}{4}[25\frac{1}{4}]$in

(63[64]cm) from beg. Fasten off. With WS facing rejoin yarn to base of last tr before back. Turn.

Next row 6ch, 1 tr into next tr, (2ch, 1 tr into next tr) 28[31] times. Turn. Work on these sts for right front. Work 2 rows in sps.

Reading RS rows from right to left and WS rows from left to right, foll chart C for motifs, set patt as foll:

1st row 6ch, 1 tr into 2nd tr, (2ch, 1 tr into next tr) 12[14] times, (2tr into next sp, 1 tr into next tr) twice, (2ch, 1 tr into next tr) 14[15] times. Turn.

Cont working from chart until the 12th row has been completed. Now cont in sps only until work measures $24\frac{3}{4}[25\frac{1}{4}]$in (63[64]cm) from beg. Fasten off.

Border

Join 17[18] sps at each side of fronts and back for shoulder seams. With RS of work facing join yarn to right front at lower edge and work 3ch, 3dc into end of base row, now work 3dc into each sp along right front, across right front top edge, across back neck, left front top edge, and left front edge, ending with 3dc into edge of base row. Fasten off.

Sleeves

Using No. 7 (1.50mm) hook make 136[142]ch.

Base row 1 tr into 5th ch from hook, 1 tr into each ch to end. Turn. 133[139] sts.

Next row 6ch, 1 tr into 4th tr, (2ch, skip next 2tr, 1 tr into next tr) to end working last tr into top of the 4ch. Turn. 44[46] sps.

Next row 6ch, 1 tr into 2nd tr, (2ch, 1 tr into next tr) to end, working last tr into 3rd of the 6ch. Turn.

Reading RS rows from right to left and WS rows from left to right, foll chart A, setting patt as foll:

1st row 6ch, 1 tr into 2nd tr, (2ch, 1 tr into next tr 20[21] times, (2tr into next sp, 1 tr into next tr) twice, (2ch, 1 tr into next tr) 21[22] times, working last tr into 3rd of the 6ch. Turn.

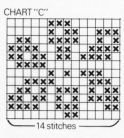

CHART "A"

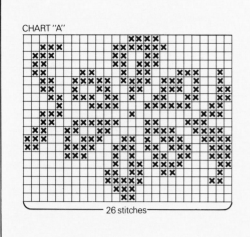

26 stitches

CHART "B"

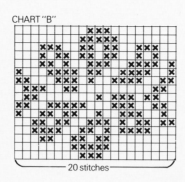

20 stitches

CHART "C"

14 stitches

KEY □ – '1SP' – (2ch, 1tr)   × = '1 BLOCK' – (3tr)

John Hutchinson

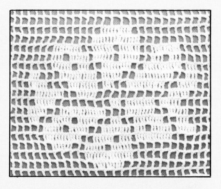

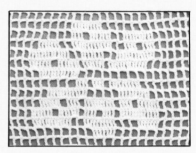

Jean Claude Volpelière

Cont working from chart until the 20th row has been completed. Work 4 rows in sps. Now set chart B as foll:
1st row 6ch, 1tr into 2nd tr, (2ch, 1tr into next tr) 20[21] times, (2tr into next sp, 1tr into next tr) 3 times, (2ch, 1tr into next tr) 20[21] times. Turn.
Cont working from chart until the 16th row has been completed.
Now cont in sps only until work measures 18in (46cm) from beg. Fasten off.

Collar
Using No. 7 (1.50mm) hook make 144ch.
Base row 1tr into 9th ch from hook, (2ch, skip next 2ch, 1tr into next ch) to end. Turn. 46 sps.
Next row 6ch, 1tr into 2nd tr, (2ch, 1tr into next tr) to end, working last tr into 3rd of the 6ch. Turn.
Rep last row 8 times more.

Border
Next row 3ch, now work 3dc into each sp along side edge, lower edge and second side edge, working 10dc into each corner sp. Fasten off.

To finish
Join sleeve seams. Set in sleeves, matching sps, join rem of side seams. Sew on collar, leaving 2¾in (7cm) of front edges free for lapels. Press seams.

KNITTING

Wild life

These tops can be worn with shorts, pants or skirts.

Zebra-striped top

Sizes
To fit 32[34:36:38]in (83[87:92:97]cm) bust.
Length, 21[21:22:22]in (53[53:56:56]cm).
Note Directions for larger sizes are in brackets []; where there is only one set of figures it applies to all sizes.

Materials
2[2:3:3] x 2oz (50g) balls of a
black sport yarn (A)
2[2:3:3] x 1oz (20g) balls of a
sport-weight metallic yarn (B)
1 pair each No. 00 and 2 (2 and 3mm) knitting needles
Size C (3.00mm) crochet hook

Gauge
36 sts and 40 rows to 4in (10cm) in striped pattern on No. 2 (3mm) needles,

Left side
Using No. 00 (2mm) needles and A, cast on 116[122:128:134] sts.
1st ribbing row *K2, P1, rep from * to last 2 sts, K2.
2nd ribbing row K1, P1, *K1, P2, rep from * to last 3 sts, K1, P1, K1.
Rep these 2 rows for 3in (7.5cm); end with a 1st row.
Next row (increase) K1, P1, K1, P2, * K twice into next st, P2, rep from * to last 3 sts, K1, P1, K1. 152[160:168:176] sts.
Change to No. 2 (3mm) needles. Beg with K row cont to work in stockinette st, foll chart No. 1. Beg reading chart from bottom right-hand side, and rep 16 sts across fabric, but for 1st and 3rd sizes

only end RS rows and beg WS rows at middle of chart. Cont in patt until work measures 10in (25cm); end with WS row.
Shape back
Bind off 4 sts at beg of next and every other row until 76[80:84:88] sts rem. Work 1 row.
Shape front
Next row K1, sl 1, K1, psso, patt to last 3 sts, K2 tog, K1.
Next row Work in patt to end. Rep last 2 rows until 6 sts rem.
Strap Change to B and cont working in stockinette st. Cast on 3 sts at beg of next 2 rows. 12 sts. Cont straight until strap measures 15in (38cm); end with WS row. Bind off.

Right side
Work as for left side, working from chart No. 2 and reversing shaping.

To finish
Press according to instructions on yarn wrapper. Join body seams. Fold straps lengthwise with seam at center and overcast.
Picot edging
Using size C (3.00mm) crochet hook and with RS facing, rejoin A to center back and work row of sc evenly all around outer edge. Turn.
Picot row *1 sc into each of next 3 sc, 3ch, sl st into top of last sc worked—picot formed—rep from * all around neck. Fasten off.

Leopard-striped top

Sizes As for zebra-striped top.
Note Directions for larger sizes are in brackets []; where there is only one set of figures it applies to all sizes.

Materials
3[3:4:4] x 2oz (50g) balls of a
yellow sport yarn (A)
4[4:5:5] x 2oz (40g) balls of a

Rod Delroy

black bulky-weight yarn (B)
1 pair each Nos. 0 and 2 (2¼ and 3mm) knitting needles
Size F (4.00mm) crochet hook

Gauge
24 sts and 24 rows to 4in (10cm)

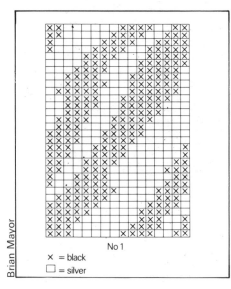

No 1
× = black
□ = silver

Brian Mayor

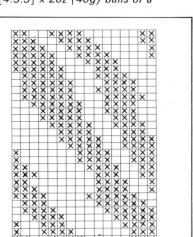

No 2

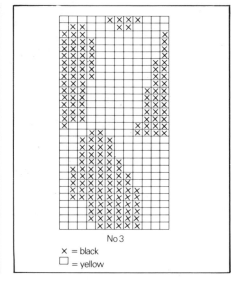

No 3
× = black
□ = yellow

spotted patt on No. 2 (3mm) needles.

Back
Using No. 0 (2¼mm) needles and A, cast on 101[107:113:119] sts.

1st ribbing row *K2, P1, rep from * to last 2 sts, K2.

2nd ribbing row K1, P1, *K1, P2, rep from * to last 3 sts, K1, P1, K1.

Rep these 2 rows for 3in (7.5cm); end with 2nd row and inc one st at end of last row. 102[108:114:120] sts.

Change to No. 2 (3mm) needles. Beg with a K row cont in stockinette st from chart No. 3 working 1st row from bottom right-hand corner and repeating 12 sts across fabric, but for 1st and 3rd sizes only end RS rows and beg WS rows at middle of chart.

Cont in patt until work measures 14[14: 14½:14½]in (35[35:37:37]cm) from beg; end with WS row.

Shape armholes
Keeping patt correct, bind off 4 sts at beg of next 2 rows.

**1st dec row K1, sl 1, K1, psso, patt to last 3 sts, K2 tog, K1.

2nd dec row K1, sl 1, P2 tog, psso, patt to last 3 sts, P2 tog tbl, K1. Rep these 2 rows until 30[32:34:36] sts rem.

Next row As first dec row.

Next row K1, sl 1, P2 tog, psso, patt to end.

Rep last 2 rows until 21[23:22:24] sts rem.

Next row Patt to last 3 sts, K2 tog, K1.

Next row K1, sl 1, P2 tog, psso, patt to end.

Rep last 2 rows until 7[7:8:8] sts rem.

Strap Using A only cont to work in stockinette st, cast on 3[3:4:4] sts at beg of next row, and 4[4:4:4] sts at beg of foll row. Cont straight until strap measures 15in (38cm) from beg; end with P row. Bind off.

Front
Work as for back to **.

1st dec row K1, sl 1, K1, psso, patt to last 3 sts, K2 tog, K1.

2nd dec row K1, P2 tog, patt to last 4 sts, P3 tog tbl, K1.

Rep these 2 rows until 30[32:34:36] sts rem.

Next row As first dec row.

Next row Patt to last 4 sts, P3 tog tbl, K1.

Rep last 2 rows until 21[23:22:24] sts rem.

Next row K1, sl 1, K1, psso, patt to end.

Next row Patt to last 4 sts, P3 tog tbl, K1.

Rep last 2 rows until 7[7:8:8] sts rem.

Strap
Work as for back.

To finish
Press or block according to yarn used. Join body seams. Fold straps lengthwise with edges at center and overcast seam together using A.

Picot edging
Using Size F (4.00mm) crochet hook and with RS facing, rejoin B to center back and work a row of sc evenly all around neck (having a multiple of 3). Turn.

Picot row * 1sc into each of next 3 sc, 3 ch, sl st into top of last sc worked— picot formed—rep from * all around neck. Fasten off.

EXTRA SPECIAL

KNITTING

Beachcomber

Be a sensation in this glamorous knitted beach dress.

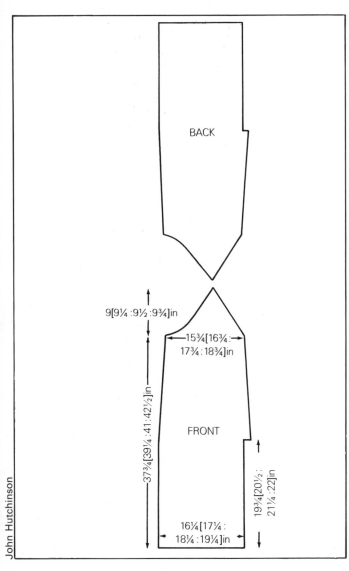

John Hutchinson

Sizes
To fit 32[34:36:38]in (83[87:92:97]cm) bust.
Length when worn, 46[48:50:52]in (117[122:127:132]cm).

Note Directions for larger sizes are in brackets []; where there is only one set of figures it applies to all sizes.

Materials
14[15:15:16]oz (380[400:420: 440]g) of a sport yarn in main color (A)
3[3:4:4]oz (60[60:80:80]g) in contrasting color (B)
1 pair each Nos. 2 and 3 (3 and 3¼mm) knitting needles
3¼yd (3m) of cord for tie (optional)
Stitch holder

Gauge
28 sts and 36 rows to 4in (10cm) in stockinette st on No. 3 (3¼mm) needles.

Front
Using No. 3 (3¼mm) needles and A, cast on 114[121:128:135] sts. Beg with a K row, cont in stockinette st until work

measures 19¾[20½:21¼:22]in (50[52:54: 56]cm); end with a P row.
Cast on 6 sts at beg of next row. 120[127:134:141] sts.
Dec one st at each end of next and every foll 50th row 5 times in all. Cont straight until work measures 37¾[39¼:41:42½]in (96[100:104:108]cm); end with a P row.
Bind off 3 sts at beg of next row, 8[8:10:11] sts at beg of next row, 2 sts at beg of next row and 7[8:10:10] sts at beg of foll row. Now dec one st at beg of next row and bind off 2 sts at beg of foll row. Dec one st at beg of next row and every alternate row 29[31:32:34] times in all and *at same time* dec one st at end on next and every foll row 56[60:62:66] times in all.
Next row K2 tog, K1. K2 tog.
Fasten off.

Back
Work as for front, reversing shaping.

Edgings
Using No. 2 (3mm) needles and B, cast on 9 sts and work in garter st (every row K) until strip fits along lower edge.

Next 2 rows K1, turn and K1.
Next 2 rows K2, turn and K2.
Next 2 rows K3, turn and K3.
Cont in this way until all sts are worked, then cont in garter st until strip fits along side edge to top of side slit. Bind off.
Work another piece the same way. Using No. 2 (3mm) needles and B cast on 9 sts and work in garter st until strip fits along shoulder edge from side seam to point.
Cut off yarn and leave sts on a holder.
Using No. 2 (3mm) needles and B, cast on 9 sts and work in garter st until strip fits along short edge.
Next row K to end, then K the sts of first strip. 18 sts.
Cont in garter st, dec one st at each end of next and every foll 4th row until 9 sts rem. Cont straight until strip measures 13¾in (35cm) from last dec, for strap.
Bind off.
Work other edging and strap the same way.

To finish
Join side seams, leaving side slit open.
Sew edgings in place. Tie straps at shoulder.

Sunshine shirring

Just right for the summer, this multi-sized, multi-purpose sundress can be teamed with its matching scarf or even worn as a full-length skirt.

Measurements
To fit sizes 10 to 14.
Bodice to hem length $38\frac{1}{2}$in (98cm).
$\frac{5}{8}$in (1.5cm) seam allowances and 2in (5cm) hem allowance are included.

Materials
$4\frac{1}{8}$yd (3.8m) of 36in (90cm)-wide fabric (subtract $\frac{7}{8}$yd [80cm] from this quantity if not making scarf)
Matching thread
Elastic thread for shirring
$3\frac{7}{8}$yd (3.5m) of $\frac{5}{8}$in (1.5cm) -wide edging for scarf
$1\frac{1}{8}$yd (1m) of $\frac{1}{2}$in (1.2cm)-wide ribbon for shoulder straps
Tailor's chalk, yardstick

Note It is uneconomical to make this garment from a wider fabric as too much is wasted when cutting out.

1 Cut out the pattern pieces following the measurement diagram and the cutting layout on page 102.

Terry Evans

2 Starting 1in (2.5cm) from one long edge, mark 18 horizontal lines on right side of each bodice (top) piece, spacing them $\frac{1}{2}$in (1.2cm) apart. These are guidelines for the shirring.

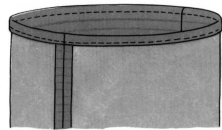

3 With right sides together and raw edges even, pin, baste and stitch side seams on both bodice and skirt. Press seams open and finish them.
Sew a double $\frac{1}{4}$in (6mm) hem around the top edge of bodice.

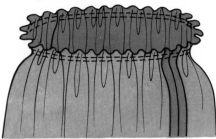

4 Within seam allowance of waist edge of skirt sew two lines of gathering stitches. Pull up the gathers to fit bodice, distributing fullness evenly.

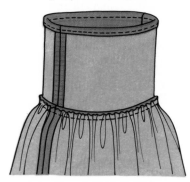

5 With right sides together and side seams aligned, pin and baste unfinished edge of bodice to skirt waist. Stitch with gathered side upward.

Jean Claude Volpelière

6 Run 18 rows of shirring around bodice, (seeTechnique tip). Take care to run stitching together accurately at beginning and end of each round.

7 Make two pieces of tubing for shoulder straps or cut two pieces of ribbon, each 19in (48cm) long. Try on dress and pin straps in place. Anchor firmly.

8 Turn up and hem lower edge of skirt.

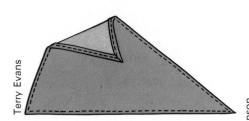

Terry Evans

9 Make a ¼in (6mm) double hem all around scarf, mitering the corners neatly, and trimming away excess fabric.

Cutting layout for 36in-wide fabric

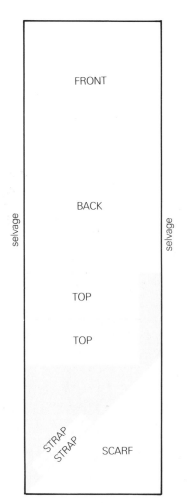

selvage

selvage

FRONT

BACK

TOP

TOP

STRAP
STRAP

SCARF

John Hutchinson

Measurement diagram

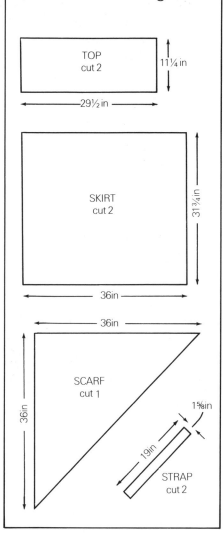

TOP
cut 2

11¼ in

29½ in

SKIRT
cut 2

31¾in

36in

36in

SCARF
cut 1

36in

1⅝in

19in

STRAP
cut 2

Technique tip

Shirring

Shirring is used to control fullness in a decorative way and consists of evenly spaced rows of gathering done with a special elastic thread which allows the fabric to stretch. It is sewn by machine, using the elastic thread in the bobbin. Shirring can be used over a whole bodice, as in this sundress, or on smaller areas such as collars, cuffs and pockets. It is also useful as a waistband on children's dresses, as it allows for growth. Prepare your sewing machine by winding a bobbin with elastic thread. You may find it preferable to wind the bobbin by hand, stretching the thread slightly.

Before starting on a garment, practice on a scrap of fabric, adjusting tension and stitch size as necessary. The longer the machine stitch, the tighter your shirring will be.

Mark the rows of shirring by drawing lines on the right side of the fabric, using either chalk or a light pencil. If you are using a plaid or striped fabric, these lines could be used as guides for stitching. A quilter attachment can also be used as a guide.

Work on the right side of the fabric, holding the fabric taut as you stitch.

When sewing additional rows, continue to hold the fabric taut to ensure that the gathers are distributed evenly. Leave about 2½in (6cm) of thread at the end of each row.

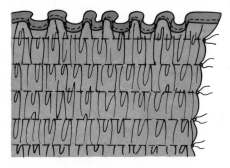

If the finished width of shirring needs adjusting, the elastic threads can be pulled up a little. Do this very gently or you will break the threads. To finish, pull threads to the wrong side and knot together.

Shoestring

Back buffer

Finished size
About 33 x 5in (85 x 12cm).

Materials
11in (28cm) piece of 36in (90cm)-wide terrycloth
5½in (14cm) piece of 36in (90cm)-wide washable interfacing
Two 3½in (9cm)-diameter wooden curtain rings
Matching sewing thread

1 Fold terrycloth in half lengthwise, matching long raw edges.
2 Place interfacing on one side of folded terrycloth, matching edges. Pin and baste other edge to fold.
3 Pin, baste and stitch long edges together, gradually increasing the seam allowance from ⅝in (1.5cm) along the center to 2¼in (6cm) at each end.
4 Trim seam allowance and turn strip right side out, enclosing interfacing.
5 Topstitch down long edges, ⅜in (1cm) from outer edge.
6 Slip one short edge of strap through one wooden ring. Pin, baste and stitch the end to the back of the strap across the strap width.
7 Repeat step 6 to join the second ring to the opposite end of the strap.

EXTRA SPECIAL SEWING

Clowning around

These clown suits can fit a variety of sizes and can be worn for almost any occasion. The children's sizes have a shirred top.

Measurements
To fit girls age three to twelve and women's sizes 10-14. Chest/bust measurements: 24[26:28:32:32½-34¼: 34¼-36¼]in (61[66:71:81:83-87: 87-92]cm). Seam allowances of ⅝in (1.5cm) have been included except on armhole edge (¼in [6mm]).
Directions for larger sizes are in brackets [ ]; if there is only one set of figures it applies to all sizes.

Suggested fabrics
Lightweight cotton or synthetics; for evening wear, crepe, satin.

Materials
1⅞[1⅞:2⅜:2⅝:3⅝:3¾]yd (1.7[1.7:2.1: 2.3:3.3:3.4]m of 36in (90cm)-wide fabric
Card of matching bias binding ⅝in (1.5cm) wide, matching thread
1⅛yd (1m) of ¼in (6mm)-wide elastic
Elastic thread (for small sizes)
⅜yd (30cm) sequin trim (optional)

1 Following the appropriate measurement diagram on page 107, cut out the suit.

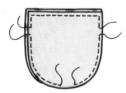

2 With right sides together, pin and baste two pocket pieces together. Stitch around two pieces, leaving a 2in (5cm) gap along lower edge and ⅜in (1cm)-long gaps 1¼in (3cm) from top of pockets (for casing). Trim seams and clip corners. Turn pocket right side out.

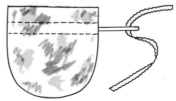

3 Topstitch across pocket ¼in (6mm) from top edge. Make a casing by sewing two lines ⅝ and 1in (1.5 and 2.5cm) from

top edge. Thread 2¾[2¾:3½:3½:4:4]in (7[7:9:9:10:10]cm) of elastic through the casing and fasten ends securely by folding under to back of pocket and stitching. Repeat for second pocket.
4 Position pockets so that lower edge is level with crotch and pockets are centered on each front section of suit. Pin and baste in place. Topstitch around edges of pocket, ¼in (6mm) from edges.

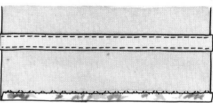

5 Turn up a ⅝in (1.5cm) hem at bottom edge of leg. Pin and baste bias binding 1⅛[1⅛:1⅝:1⅝:1⅝:1⅝]in (3[3:4:4:4:4]cm) from bottom edge. Stitch close to both edges of binding. Measure around ankle and add 1in (2.5cm) to this. Cut elastic this length. Thread through casing, gather to fit and pin ends. Repeat for other leg.
6 With right sides together, pin, baste and stitch center front seam. Clip seams and press. Repeat for center back; stitch inside leg seams, catching elastic in each seam.

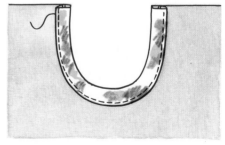

7 With right sides together, pin, baste and stitch one side of bias binding to armhole curve, ¼in (6mm) from edge. Turn binding to wrong side and slip stitch in place.
8 Fold strap lengthwise. With right sides together, baste and stitch down long side and one short end. Trim seams, turn right side out and press. Repeat for other three straps.

Jean Claude Volpelière

Terry Evans

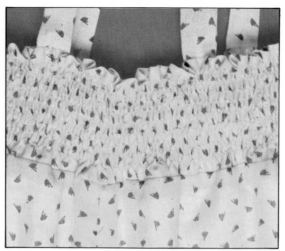

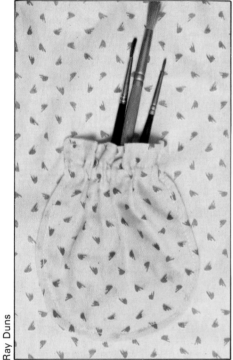

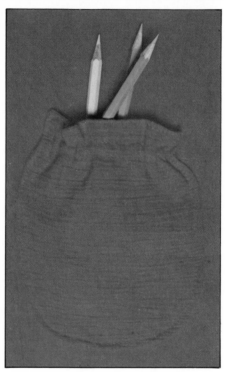

Ray Duns

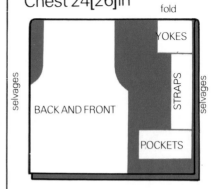

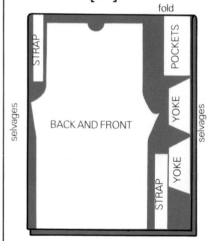

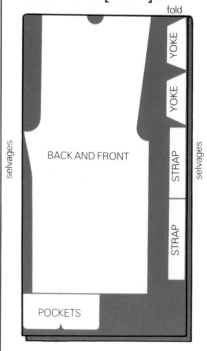

Cutting layout: 36in-wide fabric

Chest 24[26]in

fold

selvages

YOKES

STRAPS

BACK AND FRONT

POCKETS

selvages

Chest 28[32]in

fold

STRAP

POCKETS

selvages

BACK AND FRONT

YOKE

YOKE

STRAP

selvages

Sizes 10/12[12/14]in

fold

YOKE

YOKE

selvages

BACK AND FRONT

STRAP

STRAP

selvages

POCKETS

Terry Evans

Yoke for sizes 24[26]in (61[66]cm) only

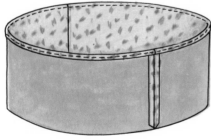

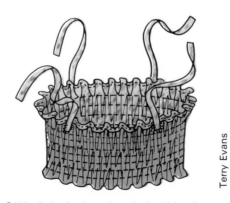

1 With right sides together, join ends of two yoke pieces together to make a circle. Make a ⅝in (1.5cm) hem at top edge of yoke.
Run a gathering thread around the lower edge of yoke, ⅝in (1.5cm) from edge. Draw up gathers to fit top edge of garment and distribute evenly. Pin, baste and stitch yoke to garment. Overcast edges of seam allowance to finish.

2 Wind elastic thread on the bobbin of the sewing machine. Leaving ⅝in (1.5cm) at top and ¾in (2cm) at bottom edge of yoke, mark and stitch shirring lines ¼in (6mm) apart (see page 102). Fasten ends securely.
Finish the open end of each strap and sew in place on inside of yoke.

Measurement diagrams

Chest 24[26]in

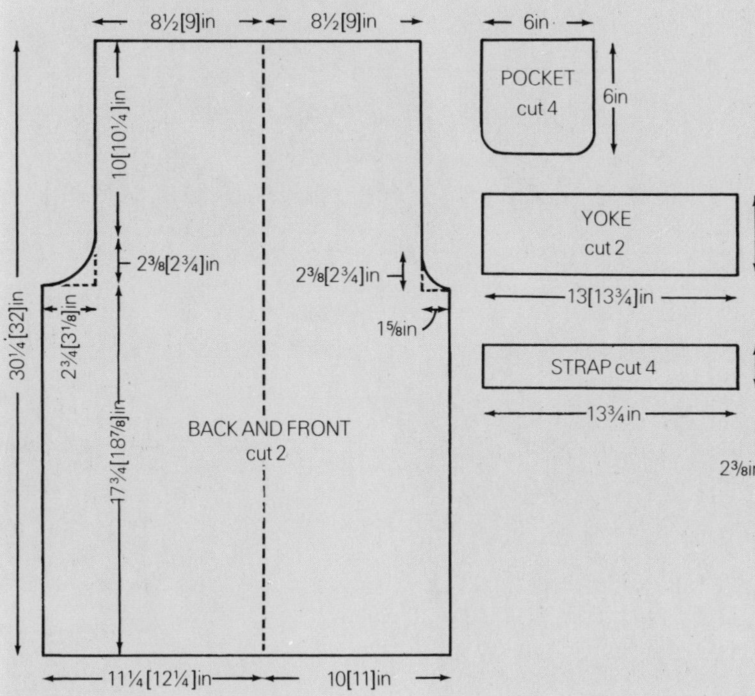

8½[9]in
8½[9]in
10[10¼]in
2⅜[2¾]in
2⅜[2¾]in
1⅝in
2¾[3⅛]in
30¼[32]in
17¾[18⅞]in
BACK AND FRONT
cut 2
11¼[12¼]in
10[11]in
6in
POCKET
cut 4
6in
YOKE
cut 2
4¼in
13[13¾]in
STRAP cut 4
2⅜in
13¾in

Sizes 10/12[12/14]in

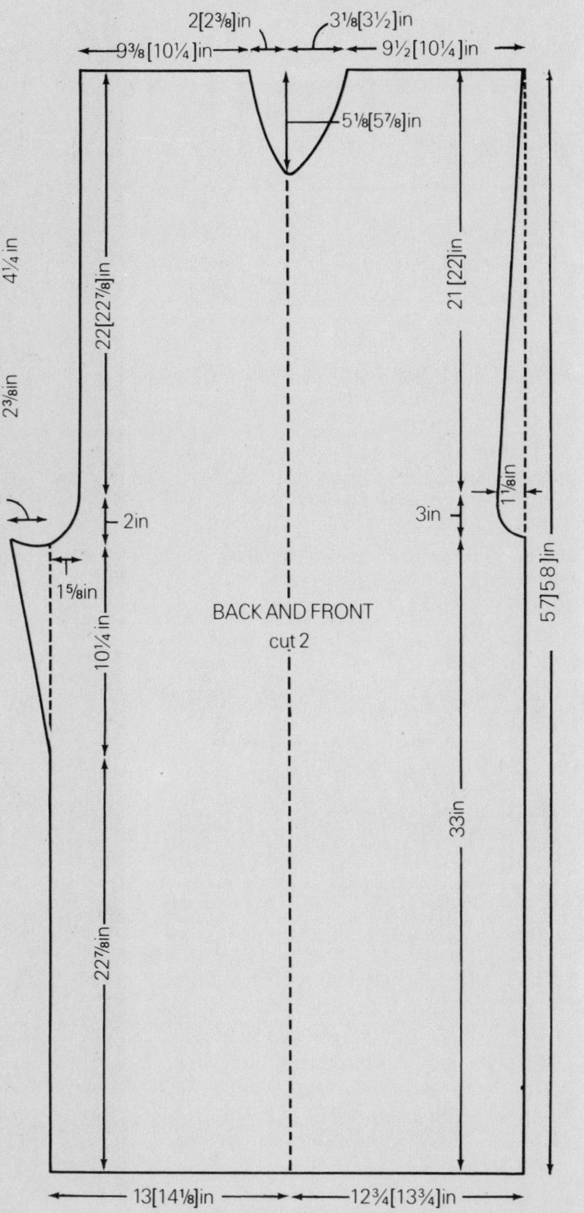

2[2⅜]in
3⅛[3½]in
9⅜[10¼]in
9½[10¼]in
5⅛[5⅞]in
22[22⅞]in
21[22]in
2⅜in
2in
1⅛in
3in
1⅝in
10¼in
BACK AND FRONT
cut 2
57[58]in
33in
22⅞in
13[14⅛]in
12¾[13¾]in

Chest 28[32]in

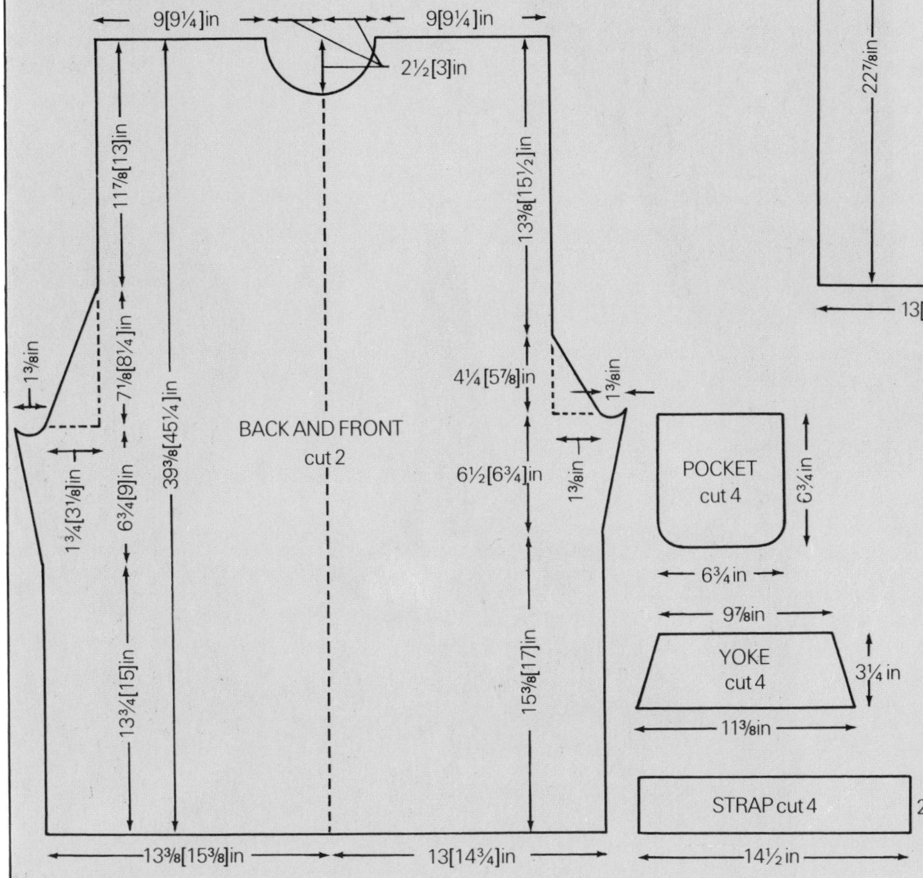

9[9¼]in
9[9¼]in
2½[3]in
11⅞[13]in
13⅜[15½]in
1⅜in
7⅛[8¼]in
4¼[5⅞]in
1⅜in
39⅜[45¼]in
BACK AND FRONT
cut 2
1¾[3⅛]in
6¾[9]in
6½[6¾]in
1⅜in
13¾[15]in
15⅜[17]in
13⅜[15⅝]in
13[14¾]in
POCKET
cut 4
6¾in
6¾in
9⅞in
YOKE
cut 4
3¼in
11⅜in
STRAP cut 4
2¾in
14½in

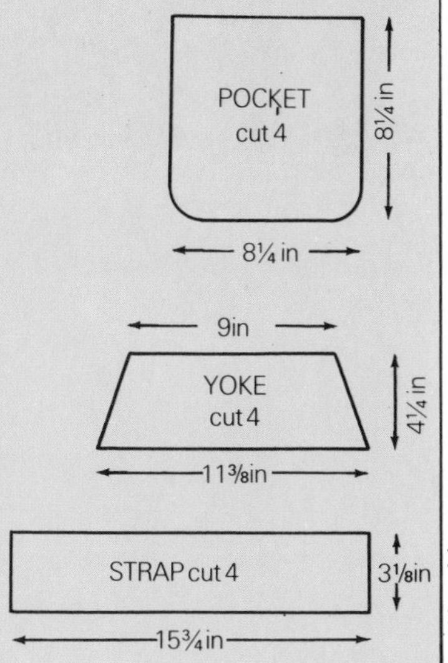

POCKET
cut 4
8¼in
8¼in
9in
YOKE
cut 4
4¼in
11⅜in
STRAP cut 4
3⅛in
15¾in

John Hutchinson

Yoke for larger sizes

1 Baste two straps to one yoke piece, $\frac{5}{8}$in (1.5cm) from corner on shorter of two long edges, with edges matching.

2 With right sides together, place another yoke piece on top. Pin, baste and stitch around the three short edges, leaving the long edge open. Clip corners, turn right side out and press. Repeat for second pair of straps and yoke.

3 Run two rows of gathering through top edge of back and front of garment, inside seam allowance. Pull up gathering to fit long (open) edge of yoke and distribute gathers evenly.

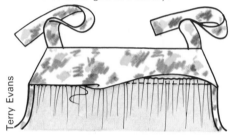

4 With right sides together, pin, baste and stitch front sections of yokes to front and back of garment. Press seam allowances and yoke upward, turn under and press seam allowance along free edge of yoke and slip stitch to inside of garment.

5 Cut optional trimming to fit yoke, adding $1\frac{1}{4}$in (3cm) for seam allowances. Hand-sew in place.

Terry Evans

Jean Claude Volpeliere

108

Homemaker

Sensible seating

If you're short of chairs and short of cash, these seats are the answer—foam blocks covered in hardwearing upholstery fabric and quilted to give them a distinctive look.

Di Lewis

Size

Each seat base is 23½in (60cm) square and 16in (40cm) deep. Each seat back is 29½in (75cm) high, 23½in (60cm) wide and 6in (15cm) deep.

Materials for two seats

6⅜yd (5.8m) of 54in (140cm)-wide upholstery fabric

2⅞yd (2.6m) of 36in (90cm)-wide medium-weight polyester batting

Two pieces of firm high-density foam 23½in (60cm) square and 14in (36cm) deep, topped with a 1½in (4cm) layer of softer foam

Two pieces of medium high-density foam 29½ × 23½in (75×60cm) and 6in (15cm) deep

3⅞yd (3.5m) of 1in (2.5cm)-wide beige touch-and-close tape

Four large sheets of tissue paper

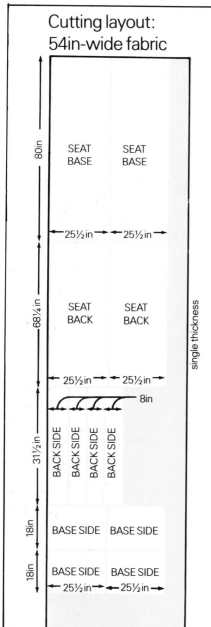

Cutting layout: 54in-wide fabric

80in

SEAT BASE   SEAT BASE

25½in   25½in

68¼in

SEAT BACK   SEAT BACK

25½in   25½in

8in

31½in

BACK SIDE   BACK SIDE   BACK SIDE   BACK SIDE

18in

BASE SIDE   BASE SIDE

18in

BASE SIDE   BASE SIDE

25½in   25½in

single thickness

Cutting out

1 Cut out the pieces for the seat bases and seat backs following the cutting plan. These measurements include 1in (2.5cm) seam allowances.

2 From batting cut out two 25½in (65cm) squares for seat bases and two rectangles 25½ × 18in (65×45cm) for seat backs.

Seat bases

Make each seat base as follows:

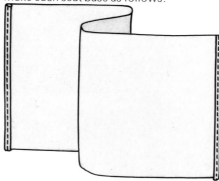

1 Turn under a ½in (1.2cm) double hem on each short edge of one seat base piece. Pin, baste and stitch hems in place.

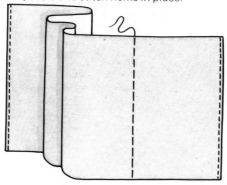

2 Measure 16in (41cm) in from one short hemmed edge on seat base and mark with a row of basting stitches. This will be the position of the first line of quilting.

3 On one sheet of tissue paper draw the quilting pattern for the seat base. Draw a rectangle 22 × 22½in (56× 57cm). Divide this rectangle with horizontal lines spaced at intervals of 2¾in (7cm).

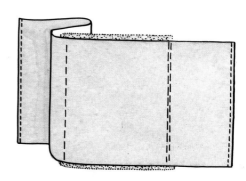

4 Pin and baste one batting square to the wrong side of the seat base, with the edge of the batting just overlapping the basted line.

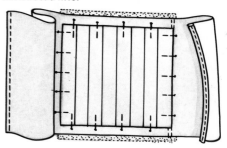

5 On the right side of the seat base, center the tissue paper pattern across the fabric, so that the first horizontal line of the pattern falls on the basted line. Pin tissue paper firmly in place.

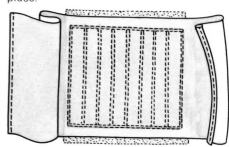

6 Using contrasting thread, machine stitch the lines of the quilting following the tissue paper pattern. Either use a twin needle or separately topstitch two lines close together. Stitch the lines across the seat first, stitching them all in the same direction. Then stitch the two outer lines. Tie off the thread ends on the wrong side of fabric.

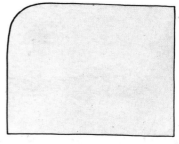

7 Round off one corner on each of two base side fabric pieces. These will be the top front corners.

John Hutchinson

Terry Evans

110

8 Turn under the 1in (2.5cm) seam allowance on the top, bottom and front side edges of the base sides. Pin and baste in place.

9 With a row of pins, mark the positions of the seamlines on the seat base fabric.

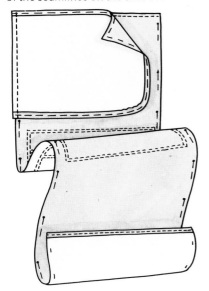

10 With right sides together, pin, baste and stitch one base side to the seat base along the back side edge only. Match the seamline to the edge of the hemmed edge of seat base and stitch only to the seamline of the seat base.

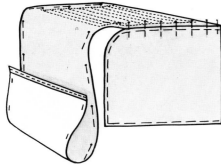

11 Working from the right side, pin the basted top edge of the base side to the seat base as shown, butting the folded edge up to the row of pins.

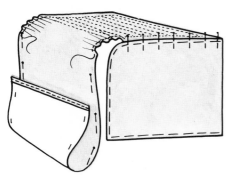

12 At the front edge of the seat base, run a 6¼in (16cm) line of gathering stitches on the seamline, starting from the end of the quilting.

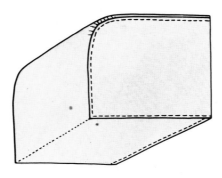

13 Continue pinning the base side in place from the opposite bottom edge, matching the hemmed edge to the seamline as before. Make a small fold in the seat base at the bottom corner of the side edge. At the gathers, pull up the gathering thread and distribute the gathers evenly to fit the rounded corner.

14 Pin and baste the base side in place. Topstitch close to the fold.

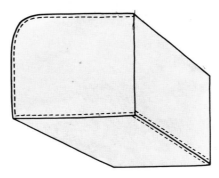

15 Repeat steps 10 to 14 for the other side of the seat base.

16 Finish the raw edges of the fabric.

17 Repeat steps 1 to 16 to make the second seat base the same way.

Seat back

1 Finish the short edges of one seat back piece and mark positions of first quilting line as for seat base, steps 1 and 2.

2 Pin and baste one batting rectangle to wrong side of seat back, with edge of batting overlapping the basted line.

3 On one sheet of tissue paper draw the quilting pattern for the seat back. Draw a rectangle 12½in (32cm) deep and 22½in (57cm) wide. Divide this rectangle with five horizontal lines spaced at 2in (5.3cm) intervals.

4 Using the top left-hand corner as the center and the distance to the second line as the radius, use a compass to draw an arc of a circle to join the top and second lines. In the same way, but with the end of the second line as a center point, draw a second arc to join the second and third lines.

5 Now, from this same point, draw a concentric arc with a 6¼in (16cm) diameter to join the second and fourth lines. Erase the portion of the horizontal line that crosses the larger arc.

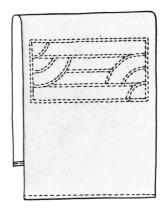

6 Repeat this design in the bottom right-hand corner. Reverse the tissue paper and trace the design so the tracing is reversed. This means that the patterns at the bottom right-hand corner will match when the seat backs are side by side.

7 Position the tissue paper pattern and work the quilting the same way as the seat base, steps 5 and 6, but stitch the arcs first, and then the horizontal lines.

8 Round off two corners on one short end of the back side pieces. This will be the top edge.

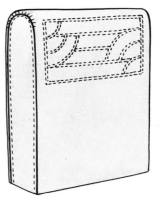

9 Stitch the back sides to the seat back as for the seat base, steps 8 to 14, but run an 8in (20cm) line of gathering stitches on each side of the seat back.

10 Repeat steps 1 to 9 to make the second seat back the same way.

Finishing

1 Insert the correct foam pieces into each of the covers. Turn in the opening edges and slip stitch together to close.

2 Cut the touch-and-close tape into six 23in (58cm)-long strips.

3 Place one seat back on top of one seat base. Separate one of the strips into its two halves. Position one half of the strip along the back of the seat base, ⅝in (1.5cm) up from base edge. Place the opposite side of the strip along the seat back in the same position. Pin, baste and sew both pieces in place.

4 Position second and third strips on the seat back and seat base the same way, spaced evenly up the base.

5 Repeat for second seat.

Terry Evans

Homemaker

Custom-made window shades

You don't need to be limited by the range of color and patterns in ready-made kits—make your own shades.

Determining the width

Window shades can be hung inside or outside the window frame. When measuring, use a wooden yardstick or steel tape, so the measurements are accurate.

Inside the frame, the fabric should completely cover the glazed window area. Measure the inside width and deduct 1in (2.5cm) from this figure to allow for the pins and fixing brackets.

For a shade fixed outside the frame, extend the shade width for 4-6in (10-15cm) at each side of the window. When you go to buy the shade kit, if you cannot find one of exactly the right width, buy one that is slightly wider, as the pole can be cut down to the measurement you need.

Preparing the wooden roller

1 Fix the brackets in place, placing the spring end of the shade on the left of the window. If the brackets are to be fixed on the front of the frame or on the wall, fix them at least 1in (2.5cm) down from the frame to allow enough clearance for the fabric-covered roller. If the roller has a large diameter, or the fabric is very thick, allow more room at the top.

2 Place the spring end of the roller in the left-hand bracket. If the roller is too long, mark the correct length with a pencil on the right-hand end of the roller.
3 Remove the roller from the bracket and saw off excess at pencil mark, working in a straight line. Fix the metal cap over the sawn end.
4 Re-fix the roller back into the brackets and check that it now fits across the window correctly.

Choosing the fabric

Pick a firm, smooth, closely woven fabric, such as cotton, linen, canvas or glazed chintz. Avoid loosely woven or thick textured fabrics. Vinyl-coated fabrics are useful as they need little sewing and are perfect for kitchens and bathrooms, since they are not affected by steam and can easily be wiped clean. You should use a fabric wide enough for your window, as seams are unattractive and will add to the bulk on the roller.

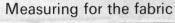

Measuring for the fabric

1 For the fabric length, measure from the fixed roller to the desired base level.
2 Add 12in (30.5cm) to this measurement, to allow for hem casing and for top fixing, so that when the shade is fully extended, the roller is still covered.
3 For the fabric width, measure the length of the roller and add 2¼in (6cm) for side hems. If using vinyl-coated fabric, omit the extra width—no side hems will be needed because the fabric does not fray.
4 If you need to join the fabric to obtain the desired width, you need to double the length of fabric.

Cutting out the fabric

It is very important that the fabric be cut out accurately; otherwise the shade will roll up unevenly and get caught in the brackets.
Always cut the fabric on the straight grain. Do not use the fabric pattern as a guide, as fabrics are often not printed straight.

1 To find the straight grain of the fabric, either tear across the fabric width or pull a weft thread across the fabric width.

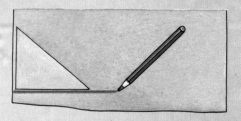

On vinyl-coated fabric use a right triangle, or other 90° angle, to make sure the short edges are cut exactly straight.

HALF WIDTH   FULL WIDTH   HALF WIDTH

Terry Evans

2 If you have to join two pieces of fabric to obtain the desired width, it is best to make two seams as shown above.

113

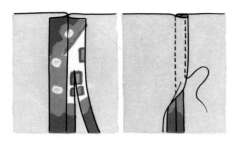

3 Cut two lengths of fabric to the same measurement. Cut one piece in half lengthwise. Join the two half pieces of fabric to each side of the main piece with flat fell seams.

4 Alternatively, if the window has a central vertical strut, seam the fabric down the center so that the seam lines up with the strut. When the shade is down, the strut masks the seam.

Finishing the fabric

1 It is important that the side hems of the shade be as flat as possible. Turn a single hem of $1\frac{1}{8}$in (3cm) to the wrong side at each long side; press and baste in place.

2 If the fabric has a tendency to ravel, first turn under $\frac{3}{8}$in (1cm) and then $\frac{3}{4}$in (2cm), press and baste in place.

3 Sew down both long edges, using a medium-to-large zig-zag stitch, in

matching thread, with the raw edge of the fabric in the center of the stitching. If your machine has no zig-zag stitch, use two rows of stitching, placing them close together.

4 For hem casing, press $\frac{5}{8}$in (1.5cm) to the wrong side, then turn up a $1\frac{1}{2}$in (4cm) hem. Press well and baste in place. Sew close to folded edge across width and down one side.

5 Remember when working with vinyl-coated fabrics to avoid pins and basting, as they will mark the fabric. Fasten down the hem casing with transparent tape before sewing. Use tissue paper between fabric and machine "teeth."

6 Cut the wooden lath (included in the shade kit) $\frac{5}{8}$in (1.5cm) shorter than fabric width. Slip the lath into the hem casing. Sew the open end closed.

7 Attach the cord and shade pull to the cord holder and fix the holder to the center of the fabric-covered lath on the underside, making sure that the cord will hang down straight.

8 Before attaching the fabric to the roller, press it well. Pay particular attention to the seams. Use a stiffening spray to give the fabric extra body.

Finishing the shade

The fabric should be attached to the roller so that it hangs next to the window, with the roller toward the room, as shown at right. It is important to take pains in attaching and rolling the fabric, so that the shade will roll up and down smoothly.

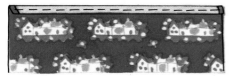

1 Turn ⅝in (1.5cm) to the right side along upper edge of fabric; press and baste.

2 Place the prepared fabric, right side up, on a table. Lay the roller across the top of the fabric, with the spring on the left-hand side, making sure that the roller is square to the fabric.

3 Attach the fabric to the roller using a staple gun or plenty of small tacks, working from the center out toward each

end. Place the staples (or tacks) at 1in (2.5cm) intervals along the marked line on the roller.

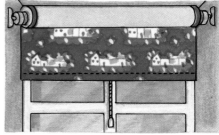

4 Roll the fabric firmly and evenly around the roller, before fixing the shade into the brackets. Pull it down to test the spring tension. If the shade does not roll up easily, pull it down again and remove from the brackets. Roll up again and replace in the brackets.

Terry Evans

Kim Sayer

115

Homemaker

Perfect patchwork

Line a small basket to hold all baby's needs or to double up as a pretty overnight case. The patchwork fabric is made of hexagons, one of the easiest patchwork shapes to use. They are sewn together by hand and, provided your preparation is accurate, the result will look professional.

Materials
One wicker picnic basket 12in (31cm) long, 10in (25cm) wide and 7in (18cm) deep
Five different printed cotton fabrics, to make 14 patches from each
$\frac{7}{8}$yd (.8m) of 36in (90cm)- wide plain fabric
White sewing thread
Bias binding
$\frac{5}{8}$yd (.5m) of 36in (90cm)-wide lightweight synthetic batting
Thin cardboard for template
Heavy paper for patches
Pencil, compass, tracing paper
Invisible sewing thread
$1\frac{3}{8}$yd (1.2m) of $\frac{3}{8}$in (1cm) elastic

Note The principles described here are used to make any patchwork based on hexagons and, by using different shaped templates, you can adapt them for a variety of patchwork formations.

Making the patches

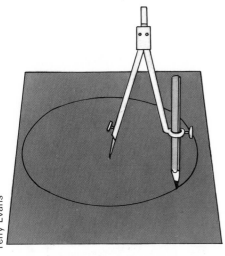

Terry Evans

1 To make a hexagonal template, draw a circle with a 1in (2.5cm) radius on the thin cardboard using pencil and compass.
2 With the compass still open at the same radius, place the compass point on the marked circle. Mark another point on the circle, 1in (2.5cm) from the compass point.

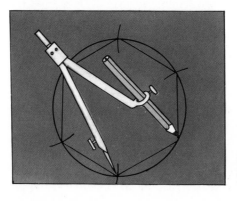

3 Move the compass point to this marked point and make another mark on the circle. Continue until the circle has been marked with six points.
4 Join these points with a ruler to make a six-sided figure, a hexagon.

5 Carefully cut out the template.

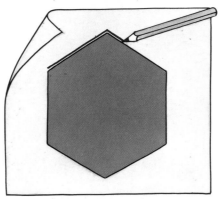

6 Place this template on heavy paper and carefully draw around it. Cut out. Accuracy is most important at this stage.
7 Repeat until you have about 70 paper hexagons.

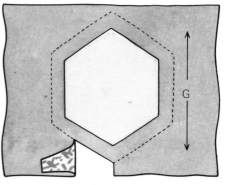

8 Using the template as a guide, mark and cut out a selection of patches from five different printed fabrics, adding $\frac{3}{8}$in (1cm) all around the template for the seams. When cutting out each fabric patch, always align two parallel sides of the template with the straight grain of the fabric.

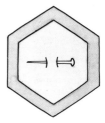

9 Next, cover the paper shapes with fabric patches by first placing a paper patch on the wrong side of a fabric patch, in the center. Pin in place.

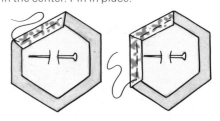

10 Fold over the $\frac{3}{8}$in (1cm) seam allowance along one side and baste through the paper patch and the fabric patch to hold. Carefully fold and turn the corner accurately, keeping the shape of the paper hexagon. Continue around patch, turning in all the edges.

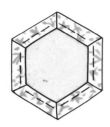

11 When basting down the seam allowances, use a medium to large stitch and do not secure the thread firmly, as the basting has to be removed when the patchwork is complete. Care must also be taken that the fabric-covered patches are accurate and that each side is of equal length; otherwise when they are sewn together they will not fit.

Sewing the patches together

Note Careful arrangement of patches is an important factor in making effective patchwork.

1 Arrange a variety of patches together, to give an interesting pattern of color and print for the inside of the basket lid. The overall shape will not be a true oblong, due to the shape formed by the hexagons when sewn together, so part of the patchwork fabric will have to be cut.

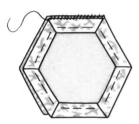

2 When the patches are arranged, place two of the adjoining patches with right sides together, matching all edges. Overcast along one of their common sides with white sewing thread. Take tiny, neat, evenly spaced stitches and pick up only a small amount of the fabric edges with each stitch. Do not sew through the papers.

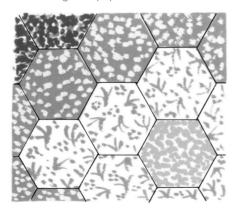

3 Continue joining the patches together in the same way, until you have sewn

Kim Sayer

enough to give a solid area of fabric, slightly larger than the lid of the basket.
4 Remove all the basting stitches. Remove the paper patches and press on the wrong side.

Lining the lid

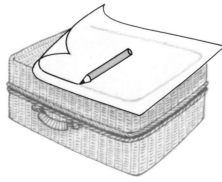

1 Place tracing paper on top of the basket lid. Mark and cut out a pattern the shape of the lid.

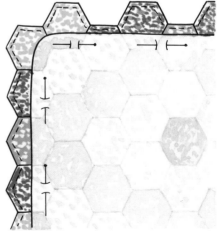

2 Center the paper pattern of the lid on your patchwork and pin it in place. Cut out.
3 Similarly, using the same tracing paper pattern, cut out one piece of batting and then cut out one piece of plain fabric for the lining.

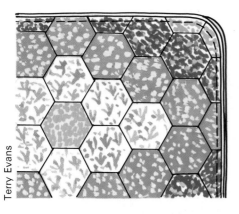

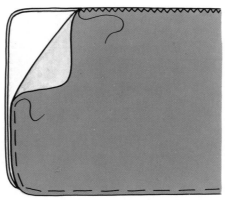

4 Sandwich the batting between the patchwork and the plain lining. Pin and baste to hold the three layers together. Zig-zag stitch around the outer edge through all three layers.

3 Sandwich the batting between the two plain fabric pieces. Pin and baste to hold the three layers together. Zig-zag stitch around the outer edge of the base, through all three layers.

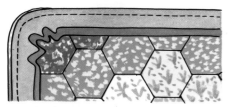

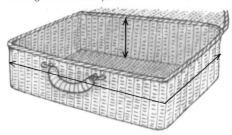

5 Next, attach bias binding around the complete outer edge: open out one edge of the binding and, with right side of binding to right side of patchwork, match this edge of binding to the raw edge of the fabric; pin and baste along binding crease. Cut off excess binding and stitch narrow edges of binding together to fit. Stitch in place.

4 Measure around the sides of the basket and the basket depth.
5 From plain fabric cut one strip the combined length of all four sides plus $\frac{3}{4}$in (2cm) seam allowance and twice the depth of the side plus $\frac{3}{4}$in (2cm) seam allowance. Piece the strip if necessary, but try to make the seam coincide with the corners of the basket if possible. Fold the fabric strip in half lengthwise, wrong sides facing, and press.
6 Cut a strip of batting $\frac{3}{4}$in (2cm) shorter than, and half the width of, the original fabric strip.

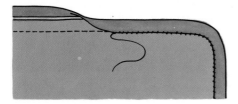

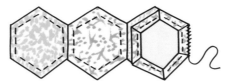

6 Fold binding over raw edges to plain fabric side; pin and baste. Slip stitch in place by hand.

7 To make a decorative band of patchwork pieces, sew a number of patches together, matching opposite sides, to form a strip the same length as the plain fabric strip.

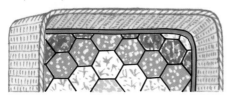

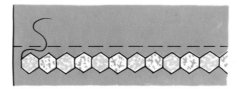

7 Place fabric inside basket lid. Using invisible thread, sew the fabric to the basket around the bound edge of the patchwork.

Lining the basket

1 Place tracing paper inside base of basket. Mark and cut out a pattern the shape of the basket base.
2 Using this pattern, cut out two pieces of plain fabric and one piece of batting.

8 Pin the patchwork strip to the plain fabric, $\frac{3}{4}$in (2cm) below the center foldline. Slip stitch along the top edge of the patches. Slip stitch along the lower edge of patches.

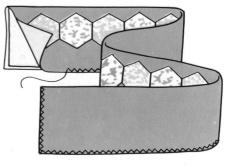

9 Sandwich the batting strip in the folded strip of fabric. Pin and baste. Zig-zag stitch along raw edges through all three layers.
10 Place strip inside basket and pin the two short ends together to fit correctly. Remove from basket, and pin, baste and stitch the seam. Press seam flat.

Terry Evans

12 Pin, baste and stitch seam. Remove all basting stitches.

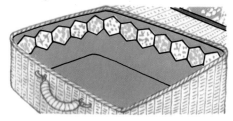

13 Place fabric lining inside basket. Using invisible thread, sew top edge of lining to the rim of the basket.

Elastic holding band

1 Cut a strip of elastic, long enough when unstretched to go around the four sides of the basket.

2 Cut enough $1\frac{1}{2}$in (4cm) -wide strips of plain cotton to make, when joined together, one long strip twice the length of the elastic.

3 Fold the fabric in half lengthwise, right sides together. Pin, baste and stitch long edge to form a $\frac{5}{8}$in (1.5cm) -wide channel. Turn fabric channel right side out.

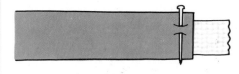

4 Thread elastic through the fabric channel, pinning one end so that it does not slip inside the channel during threading.

Kim Sayer

11 Pin and baste side lining to base lining, right sides facing, taking care to produce neatly curved corners to match the shape of the basket. Place lining inside basket to ensure a good fit, adjusting the seam if necessary.

5 Join the two ends of elastic together firmly.

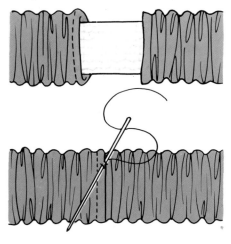

6 Fold under a narrow hem at one end of the fabric channel. Slip the other end of the fabric tube inside this end. Pin, baste and slip stitch ends together to finish, so forming the holding band. Distribute the fullness of the gathers evenly.

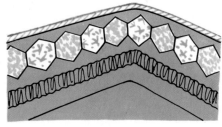

7 Pin the holding band to each corner of the basket, just under the row of patchwork. Pin again in the middle of each of the two long sides.

8 Using invisible thread, sew the band in place, sewing through the elastic, the fabric lining and the basket, to make sure that it is firmly attached.

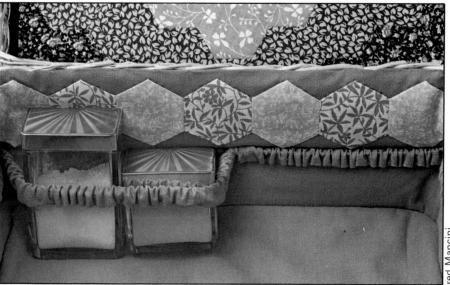

Fred Mancini

Homemaker

Lovable bear

Every child must have a teddy bear. Ours is traditional from his furry ears to his leather paws. Made from cuddly brown fur fabric, he has a gentle growl that will soothe away any woes.

Kim Sayer

Size

The teddy bear is about 23½in (60cm) tall. Seam allowances of ⅜in (1cm) have been included throughout.

Materials

1⅛yd (1m) of 48in (122cm)-wide medium-brown fur fabric
Piece of leather 13½ × 4½in (34×11cm)
Four 1in (3cm) joints*
One 1¼in (3.5cm) joint*
One pair of ⅝in (1.5cm) diameter brown safety eyes*
Black stranded embroidery floss
One "growler"*
6in (15cm) square of lightweight fabric
Suitable stuffing material
Matching thread; darning needle
Round-nosed pliers
*available from notions counters

Cutting out

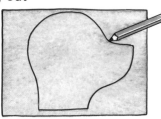

1 Using tracing paper and a sharp pencil trace pattern pieces shown on pages 122 and 123. Cut out each piece.
2 Cut out all pieces in the appropriate fabrics, the number of times stated.

Head

1 Place the head gusset between the two head pieces with right sides together, placing it between the nose and the back of the neck, matching points A and B. Pin, baste and stitch in place along both seams.

2 Pin, baste and stitch head together from point of nose (A) to neck edge.

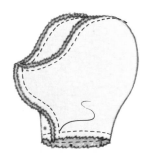

3 Run a gathering thread around neck edge. Turn head right side out.
4 Insert safety eyes into head. Find the most appealing position and fix in place permanently.
5 Stuff head firmly.

6 For the neck joint, use larger joint and insert one disk with cotter pin and washer inside neck opening of stuffed head. Put second washer of joint to one side. Pack stuffing all around the disk, so the disk cannot be felt from the outside. Pull up the gathering thread around the neck and anchor it firmly.

7 Using six strands of black embroidery floss, embroider nose in satin stitch and mouth in back stitch. Position V-shaped nose at point A.

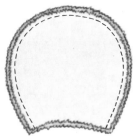

8 Match two ear pieces with right sides together. Pin, baste and stitch around curved edge, leaving bottom edge open. Turn ear right side out.

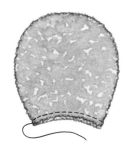

9 Turn in lower edges of ear. Pin, baste and run a line of gathering around lower edge. Pull gathering thread up tight and fasten off.
10 Repeat steps 8 and 9 to make second ear.
11 Pin ears on the head finding the best position. Baste and sew firmly in place.

Body and limbs

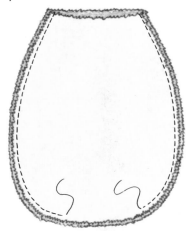

1 Place two body pieces together, right sides facing. Pin, baste and stitch around body from one side of neck to the other, leaving a 2½in (6cm) opening in the bottom. Turn body right side out.
2 Turn in neck edge of body. Pin, baste and run a line of gathering around neck. Pull up gathering and fasten off.
3 Insert cotter pin of head joint through the hole formed by the gathering at the top of the body. Push on the second disk and washer from the inside of the body. Turn the body upside down and place on head. Using round-nosed pliers, bend cotter pin so that the head is held securely. Put head and body to one side.

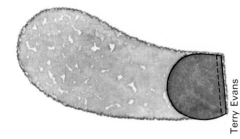

4 Match straight edge of one leather paw to straight edge of one inner arm, right sides together. Pin, baste and stitch in place.

Terry Evans

121

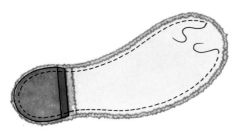

5 Match inner arm to outer arm with right sides together. Pin, baste and stitch all around, leaving a 2½in (6cm) opening at the shoulder end.
6 Turn arm right side out. Stuff to within 1¼in (3.5cm) of top.
7 To fix joint in place, use one of the smaller joints and push one disk and cotter pin through the inner arm at position marked. Finish stuffing the arm firmly, keeping top part fairly flat. Turn in open edges and slip stitch together to close.
8 Repeat steps 4 to 7 to make second arm.

9 Place two leg pieces together, right sides facing. Pin, baste and stitch around leg from heel to front of toe, leaving a 3in (7.5cm) opening in the top and leaving the base of the foot open.

Terry Evans

10 Place a leather sole in base opening of the leg. Pin, baste and stitch the sole in place. Turn leg right side out.
11 Stuff the leg to within 1¼in (3.5cm) of top. Position half of the third small joint; and close as for arm, step 7.
12 Repeat steps 9 to 11 to make the second leg.
13 Push the cotter pins of both arms through marked positions on body. Add second disk and washers and anchor as for head.

14 Stuff the upper body firmly, especially around the neck, so that the joint disk in the neck cannot be felt from the outside.

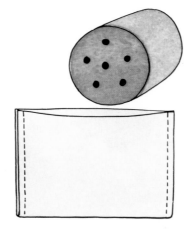

15 To make a small bag to hold the growler in place inside the body, fold the 6in (15cm) square of lightweight fabric in half. Pin, baste and stitch short edges. Turn right side out. Slip growler inside bag, turn in remaining edges and slip stitch together.
16 Place the bag containing the growler inside the body, with the holes of the growler against the center back seam. Sew the fabric surrounding the growler to the center back seam of the bear to anchor the growler. Pack stuffing firmly around the growler, so that it will stay in place.
17 Fasten the legs to body the same way as for arms, step 13.
18 Finish stuffing the bear firmly. Turn in opening edges in the base of the bear's body and slip stitch together.

19 Using six strands of black embroidery floss, embroider four "claws" on each of the four paws, sewing the claws at the ends halfway over the edges of the leather pads.

Finishing the teddy

1 Using the blunt end of a darning needle, pull out any fur pile that was caught in while sewing the seams. This will cover the seamlines.
2 Give the teddy a good brushing.

John Hutchinson

front

B

FOOT SOLE
cut 2 in LEATHER

B

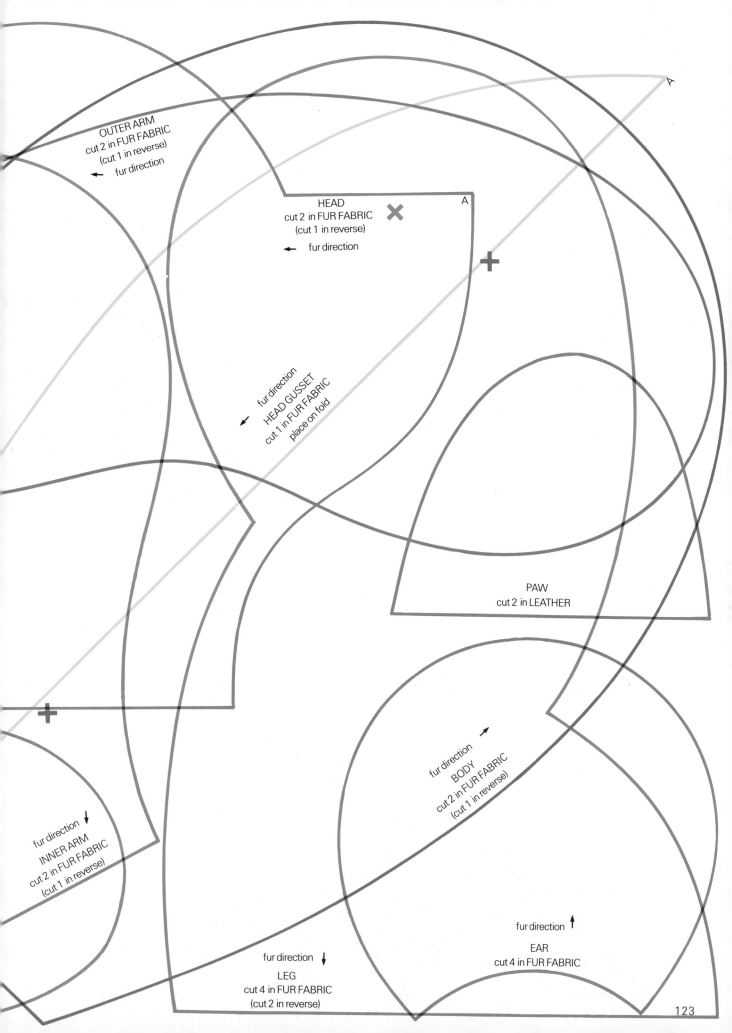

OUTER ARM
cut 2 in FUR FABRIC
(cut 1 in reverse)
← fur direction

HEAD
cut 2 in FUR FABRIC
(cut 1 in reverse)
← fur direction

A

fur direction
HEAD GUSSET
cut 1 in FUR FABRIC
place on fold

PAW
cut 2 in LEATHER

fur direction
BODY
cut 2 in FUR FABRIC
(cut 1 in reverse)

fur direction
INNER ARM
cut 2 in FUR FABRIC
(cut 1 in reverse)

fur direction ↑
EAR
cut 4 in FUR FABRIC

fur direction ↓
LEG
cut 4 in FUR FABRIC
(cut 2 in reverse)

123

Homemaker

Initially yours

Give a touch of class to your personal belongings with monograms, worked by hand or by machine. We've provided alphabets in two different styles—choose the one that best suits the article you're decorating.

Materials
Garment or household item which lends itself to this kind of decoration—we chose a book cover, pillowcases and towels
Stranded embroidery floss
Thread
Tracing paper
Dressmaker's carbon paper
Embroidery hoop

For the book cover: a piece of fabric 2in (5cm) larger than the total area of the book binding
Fabric glue
Felt, same size as book binding

Note The letters can be traced from the page, making them the same size. Or you can enlarge them, following the instructions given overleaf.

Gary Warren

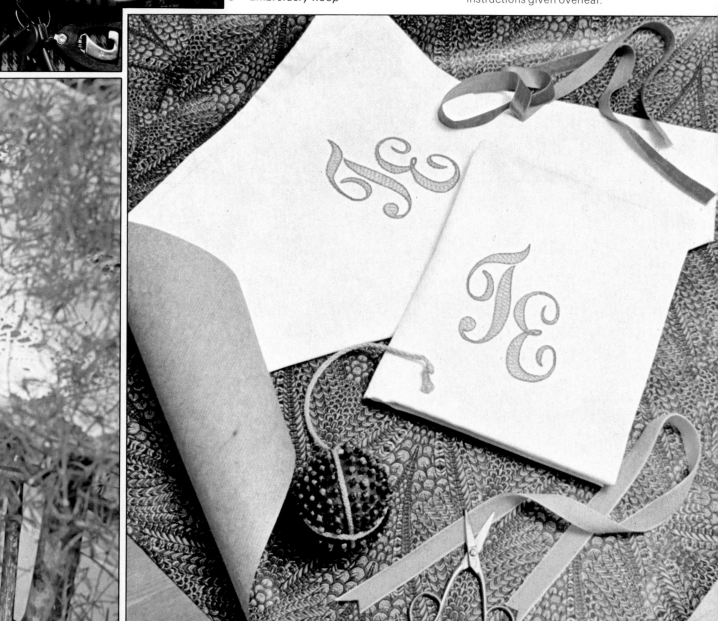

ABCDEFGHIJ
KLMNOPQR
STUVWXYZ

ABCDEFGHI
JKLMNOPQR
STUVWXYZ

abcdefgh
ijklmnopq
rstuvwxyz

abcdefghij

klmnopqrs

tuvwxyz

To enlarge the initials

The letters shown here are $\frac{3}{4}$in (2cm) tall, but they can be enlarged to any size you wish.

There is a grid of $\frac{1}{8}$in (3mm) squares over the letters on this page. To make them larger, draw a square grid the size you need on a piece of paper, using a ruler as a guide. For example, for letters four times the original size, the grid squares must be four times larger. Copy the letters onto your enlarged grid, positioning each part of the letter on the square which corresponds to the equivalent square on the original grid.

Book cover

1 Trace the letters or initials you wish to embroider, in the correct order, aligning them evenly. (If you wish, enlarge the letters first.)

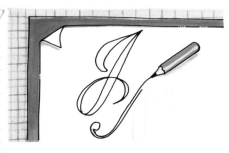

2 Using dressmaker's carbon paper, transfer the letters onto the fabric in the position you have chosen for them. Remember to allow a margin of about 2in (5cm) for turning under later.

Terry Evans

127